TURNING DREAMS TO REALITY

SREI'S INFRASTRUCTURE JOURNEY

Turning Dreams to Reality: Srei's Infrastructure Journey is a graphic novel essaying the extremely interesting and exciting voyage that Srei's founders traversed beginning in the year 1989, twenty-seven years ago.

The history of this unique journey will bear testimony to the fact that the infrastructure development of India over the last couple of decades has been truly remarkable and can be emulated by other countries, both developed and developing. India has been the vanguard of public-private partnerships for the development of infrastructure. A pioneer of such partnerships, Srei, inspite of hurdles, has been immensely successful.

This read will be both quick and gripping.

Published on behalf of Srei by
Rupa Publications India Pvt. Ltd 2017
7/16, Ansari Road, Daryaganj
New Delhi 110002

Sales centres:

Allahabad Bengaluru Chennai
Hyderabad Jaipur Kathmandu
Kolkata Mumbai

Designed and created by Atomic Labs
Creative: Retwick Roy
Text: Debayan Dasgupta
contact@atomiclabs.in
www.atomiclabs.in

ISBN: 978-81-291-4242-9

First impression 2017

Printed at Lustra Print Process, Haryana

India in the 1980's was in the midst of an economic turmoil. Infrastructure in general was at an all time low with negligible private investment. The government recognized a few key sectors, such as civil aviation, railways, power and transport, that needed critical attention.
DI-033425

Civil aviation is one of the critical sectors for the economic growth of a country. India's inadequate airport capacity was a major challenge and developing the tier 1 airports was an area of immediate focus.
Huge delays again today...the backlog of flights is piling up.
Not just passenger flights, the freight sector is lagging too.

Similarly, Indian Railways, one of the largest railway networks in the world was facing similar issues due to outdated technology, lack of government spending and huge losses owing to inefficiency.
We should dedicate a separate corridor for freight mobilization and prevent further losses.

The power and transport sectors, two key indicators of socio-economic development, were also in acute need of attention.

In 1992, the mounting fiscal deficits, the ever increasing non-planned expediture, loss-making public sector undertakings, and worsening current account deficits continued to be areas of serious concern. To tackle these issues, the planning commission prepared a proposal for the Finance Minister.

In the midst of this economic turmoil, far away from the corridors of power in New Delhi, businessman Hari Prasad Kanoria was successfully running the Bengal Flour Mills, which he had bought from Balmer Lawrie in Calcutta.

Apart from managing the Bengal Flour Mills, Hari Prasad was also running a steel and aluminium utensils plant that he set up in 1967 in Patna, Bihar.
STRIKE
However, like every Indian entrepreneur at the time, Hari Prasad was facing several challenges including union strikes and other macro economic factors. However, he was determined to beat the system and move forward in business endeavours.

Hari Prasad's eldest son, Hemant, had just finished his schooling at La Martiniere for Boys, Calcutta. At the age of seventeen, he joined his father in the flour mill business, while pursuing his higher education at St Xaviers College. He was also paralelly studying chartered and cost accountancy.

Young Hemant learnt the ropes quickly. In 1981, he was given his first assignment—to manage two flour mills the family had acquired in West Bengal. One was sick, while the other had shut down completely. His task was to revive both and make them profitable, as guided by his father.

Hemant worked diligently and successfully revived the mills. He also involved himself in learning about other important industries in India. But clouds were looming on the horizon...

On 11 October 1986, Hari Prasad lost his father, Kedarnath Kanoria. At the same time, the business was facing a stiff challenge.
Hemant, have you heard?
What is it?
There has been a sudden change in government policy. They have stopped the supply of wheat. Our flour mills are going to take a hit.

This is going to be very tough.

Where will we get our supply from?

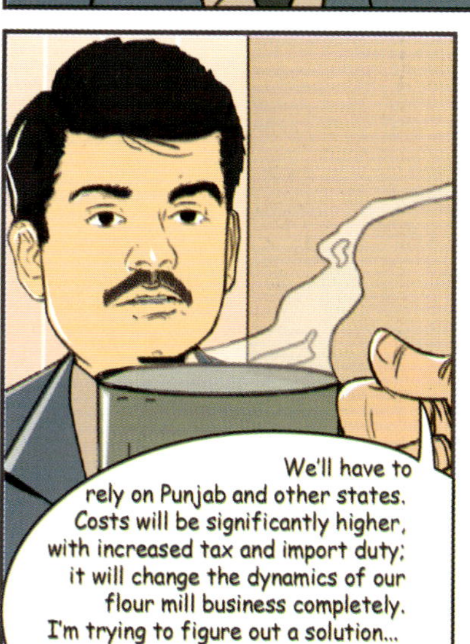
We'll have to rely on Punjab and other states. Costs will be significantly higher, with increased tax and import duty; it will change the dynamics of our flour mill business completely. I'm trying to figure out a solution...

These are difficult times. Though we will continue supply and trading, we should look at other areas. I was thinking of export and manufacturing. I am meeting an old friend and business consultant to discuss this.

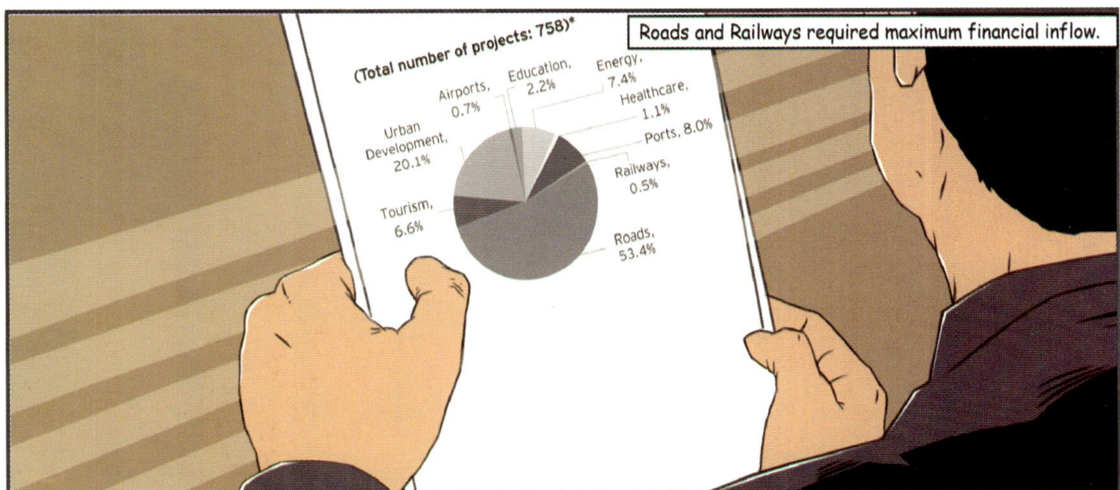

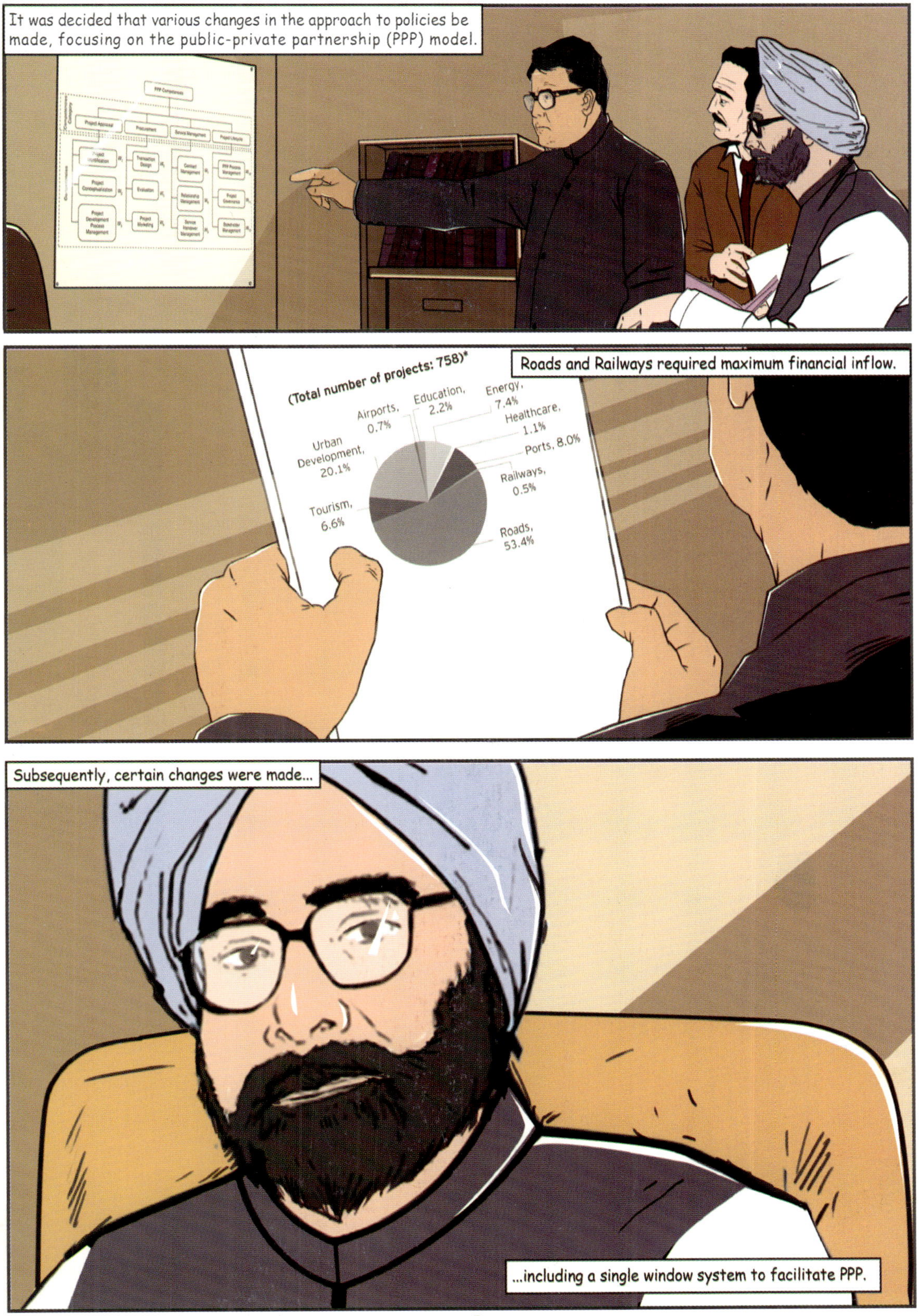

Subsequently, certain changes were made...

...including a single window system to facilitate PPP.

Next day, in a meeting with the consultant...

Hari ji, I must admit that you are quite a fighter. Even so, I would advise against exploring new avenues at this critical time.

I have faith in God and my instinct tells me to proceed. I am working on a plan.

The plan took shape very shortly...

So you think we should continue running the mills despite the current situation? I have spoken to a few industry experts regarding export-import. They seem optimistic.

I trust my instincts more than expert advice. We will work hard on our existing business. We can surely explore other areas at the same time.

THE TIMES OF INDIA

Rail Wreck Fatal To 20

Missing Order Blamed For Mountain Crash

But there is a lot left to be improved. Otherwise, mishaps will continue to happen. We have faulty track lanes, overcrowded trains, but the good thing is that the government is now inviting private players to contribute.

ROSTOV
True to Hari Prasad's decision, the family now diversified into export-import.

Shortly afterwards, Hemant's younger brother, Sunil, joined the family business, having completed his chartered accountancy course in 1987.
Sunil told Hemant that he wanted to explore opportunities in infrastructure equipment financing.
We need to move fast to be the pioneer. What do you feel about the country's present scenario?
Well, there are regulatory issues and a lack of economic reforms.

Correct! And the other two major issues are poor liquidity and poor infrastructure.
After much contemplation, in 1989, the Kanorias decided to shift their business focus altogether; they knew that the only way forward for India would be to encourage private sector participation in infrastructure, so they set out to finance project development and equipment.

Later...
Father, I feel India's deficient infrastructure will become a goldmine of opportunities in the near future. If we can carve out a unique space for ourselves, we will benefit a great deal and also contribute to the country's development.
Financing of infrastructure equipment will open up opportunities for contractors to get loans and lease equipment, which the banks are not financing.
Sounds like you both have a good strategy.

Next week...
Sunil shared his business plan with his professor, Vinod Kothari, an expert on hire-purchase and leasing, who offered Sunil some study material.

Sunil started studying the material extensively.

From his research, he figured out that the domain of hire-purchase and leasing at that point was dominated by the likes of Ashok Leyland...
ASHOK LEYLAN

Automobile was the buzzword in the hire-purchase and leasing sector.

But, like their father, the brothers trusted their intuition more than they trusted conventional practices...
Sunil, leasing here is dominated by players from the auto industry; it's already saturated. We need to find a different domain...

What do you have in mind ?

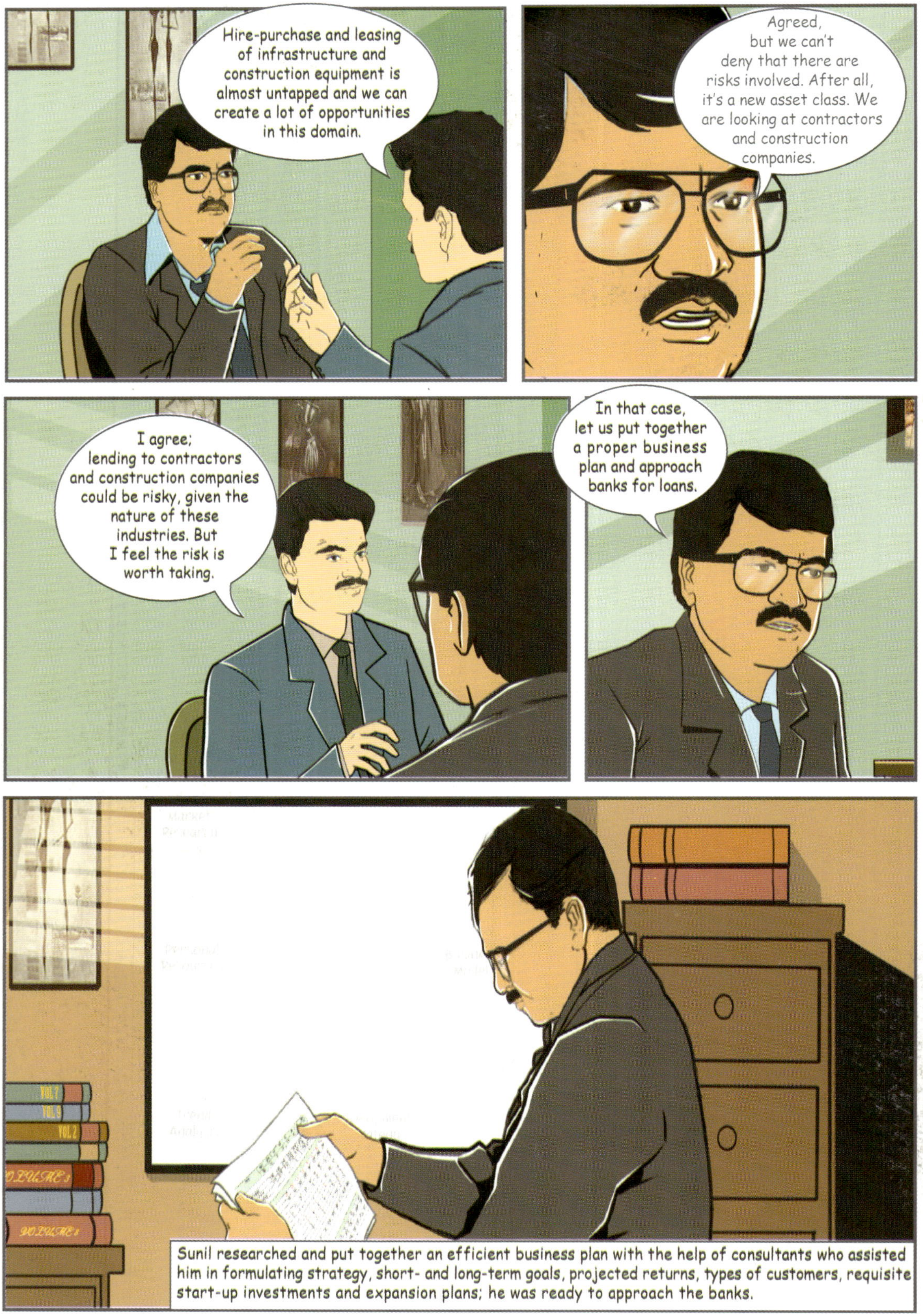

Sunil researched and put together an efficient business plan with the help of consultants who assisted him in formulating strategy, short- and long-term goals, projected returns, types of customers, requisite start-up investments and expansion plans; he was ready to approach the banks.

But things turned out to be way more difficult than they had thought...
The brothers tried very hard, but it was tough to get funding in those days...
THE STATESMAN
One of the first banks to help them was Canara Bank, which granted them a loan of Rs 5 lakh. This was followed by a loan of Rs 25 lakh from Allahabad Bank.
However, Hemant and Sunil were relentless in their efforts and their hard work finally paid off...
Meanwhile, the government began reforming infrastructure investment policies; economic liberalization was on the horizon...

Having identified infrastructure financing as their core business area, the Kanoria family began operations in 1989. The seeds of Sri Radha Krishna Export Import Industries (Srei) were sown during this time.
The name 'Srei' is derived from the Sanskrit word 'Sre'ya' and has multiple meanings, including auspicious, credit and merit.
SREI
But the most relevant meaning originates from the word 'sreshtha', meaning 'the first' or 'best'. Incidentally, it also served as an abbreviation for Sri Radha Krishna Export Import Industries.
With a modest investment, Hemant and Sunil, under the able guidance of Hari Prasad Kanoria, made an ambitious entry into the infrastructure equipment financing domain. The business was challenging. It required experience, knowledge and expertise, and substantial investment.

Driven by an indomitable spirit and firm resolve, Hemant and Sunil started working on Srei's vision and strategy with great diligence and focus.
Before anything else, we need to set our policies in place...
If Srei can become part of the infrastucture growth story, it will help the nation grow.
Later...
Father, in order to create a distinct space for ourselves in the infrastructure sector, I feel that we need to come up with an innovative business model.
Hmm... So what's innovation according to you? Is it breaking conventions and doing things differently?

Innovation is not just about doing things differently; it's about identifying and applying better solutions to meet new requirements. This will lead us towards continuous and sustainable growth.
Customer orientation and employee engagement will be our key focus areas.

We will focus on innovation, but the first step is securing adequate liquidity, assets and tie-ups with banks—here and abroad. Let us network with bankers to identify investors and also with the industry people to identify customers.

Hemant and Sunil engaged themselves in extensive research on their target sector. During this time, their youngest brother, Sujit, joined them.

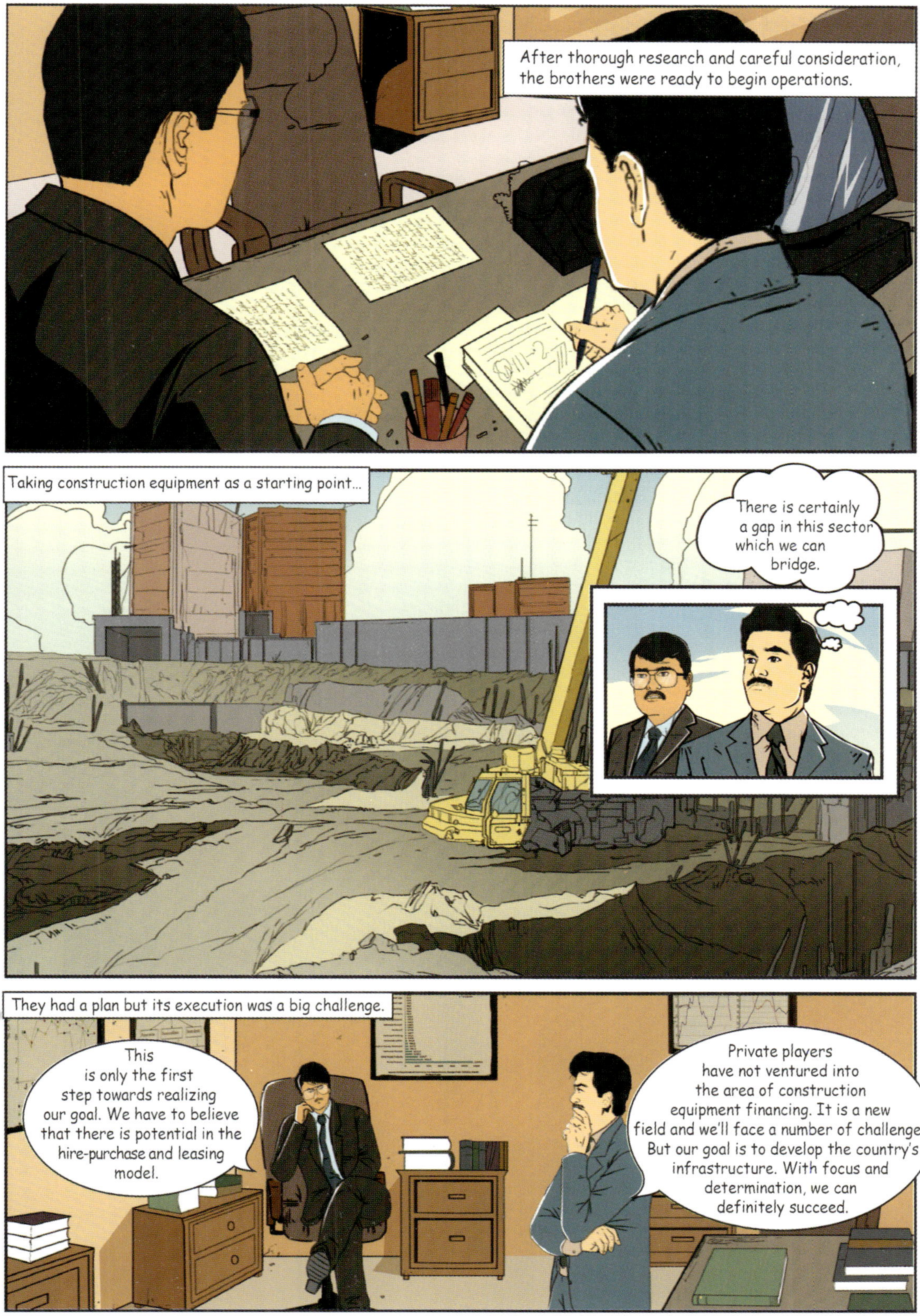

Taking construction equipment as a starting point...

There is certainly a gap in this sector which we can bridge.

Next day at breakfast...
So how far did you progress with your plan?

We have given it a thought. We are laying emphasis on networking. We feel our approach needs to be unique as it's pretty much uncharted territory.
That's good, but include conventional wisdom in your approach. This will help you remain stable during trying times.

At the end of the discussion, Hari Prasad had an advice for his sons...
I suggest you register Srei with the Lease and Hire Purchase Association. That will help you immensely.

In the early 1990s, Srei got registered with the Lease and Hire Purchase Association.

They started attending council meetings and had numerous discussions with the council heads...
They talked about risk management techniques and industry best practices.

From these meetings, Hemant and Sunil developed a deeper knowledge and insight on the subject.

They started planning their goals and objectives more effectively.

At this point Srei had begun to expand.
Srei's Kolkata office.

To gain customer confidence, we need to set ourselves apart from our competitors and banks.
Yes; we need to have a focused customer-centric approach.

We'll lend at higher interest rates but make up for that by processing loans faster and more efficiently. Customers will save money, time and man-hours on their projects.
We will also offer them business, finance and technical advice to help them succeed.

The next day, Hemant came up with a suggestion.
Our lending structure offers small business owners a real advantage over banks.
Yes; we will add value by offering them equipment servicing, maintenance information, and technical know-how.
The fact that we'll agree to work with them on the basis of their cash flow statement is in itself a huge advantage for these small contractors. We'll come across as a company that understands their needs and helps them successfully execute projects, thereby ensuring profitability.
Flexibility is essential to our business offerings. We will lend to those whom the banks refuse.
The brothers explained their business model to S. Bhattacharya and S.K. Mitra of Larsen & Toubro (L&T) at a conclave at the Calcutta Chamber of Commerce, where Hari Prasad Kanoria had enjoyed a long and illustrious tenure as president.
MCMXVU

Hemant and Sunil firmly believed in the famous quote by Paulo Coelho: 'When you want something, all the universe conspires in helping you to achieve it.' Sure enough, good news was on the way.

TRING!!!
TRING!!!

Hello, Hemant! I'm calling from Larsen & Toubro. I wish to discuss a proposition. We make and sell poclain excavators, and a client urgently needs one.

Okay. How would you like us to help you?

We would like you to finance this equipment to the contractor.

A giant like L&T is our first prospective partner. That's a great thing.

Hari Prasad was proud to see his sons taking on such a big challenge.
Indeed! We must try our best to make the most of this opportunity.

Hemant and Sunil conducted extensive research for financing their first project...
They spent endless hours in reading documents and reports on the mining industry.

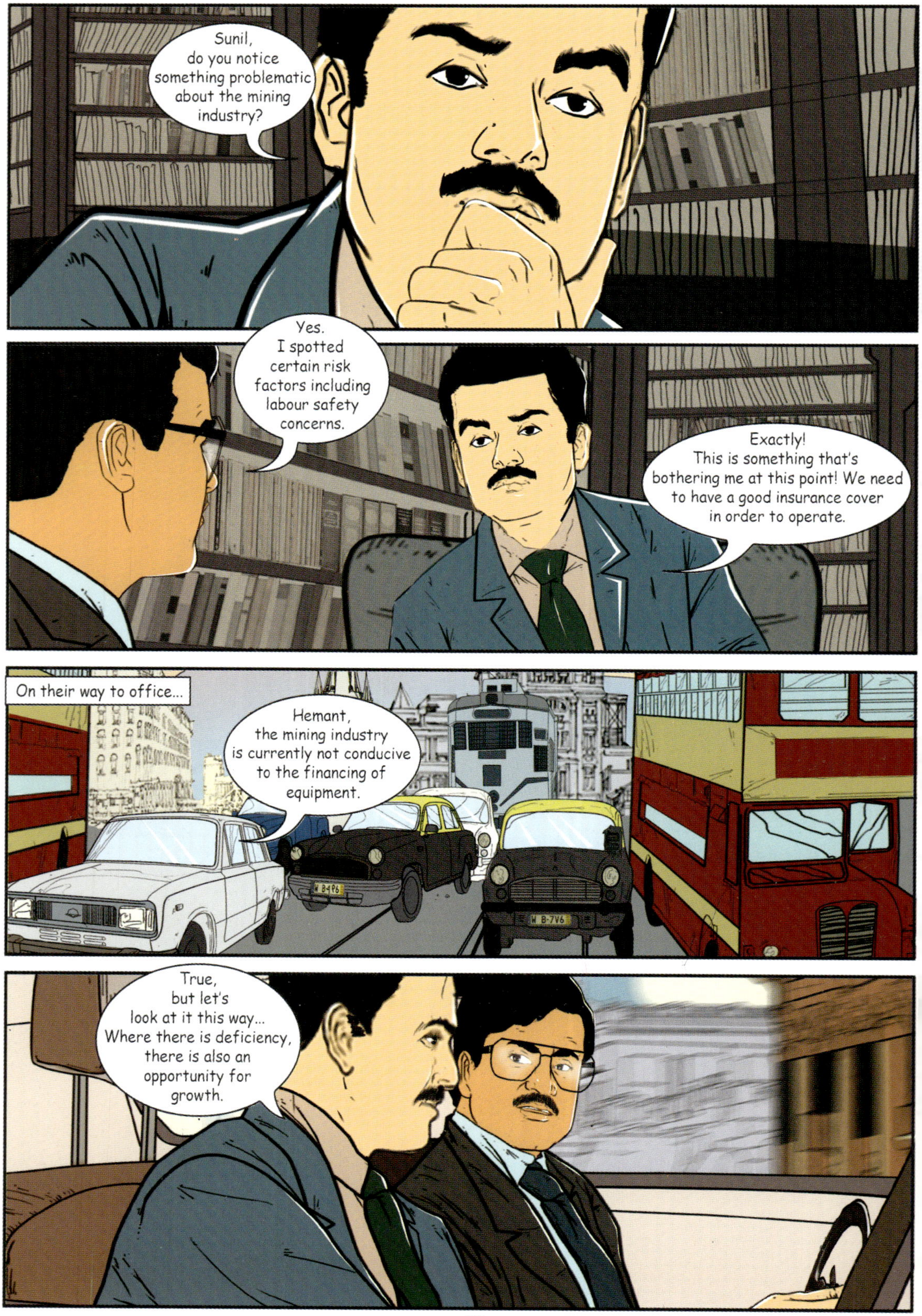

Sunil, do you notice something problematic about the mining industry?

Yes. I spotted certain risk factors including labour safety concerns.

Exactly! This is something that's bothering me at this point! We need to have a good insurance cover in order to operate.

Next day, at breakfast, the brothers continued the discussion...
L&T is one of the industry leaders.
If Srei associates itself with L&T in this project, it's a win-win situation for all...
It will enable small contractors to access funds and customers to enjoy increased benefits from mechanization. Small contractors usually cannot provide financial statements based on which credit decisions can be taken.
We can go to them and explain how, with the use of L&T equipment, their time period for completing the job will reduce from five years to three years. What's more, their rates won't fall, allowing them to make substantial profits. The client can pay back the interest and equipment cost within a year, and begin making a profit from the second year itself.
Hmm... The solution will stem from asset-based leasing. The focus will be on the generation of cash in the future.

The brothers successfully explained the 'Srei advantage' to the contractors as they sealed their first project with L&T.

Hemant and Sunil got actively involved with the manufacturers and became closely associated with the functioning of the clients. Srei went on to establish a great association with L&T in the coming years.

This eventually led Srei to pioneer the concept of partnering with its clients as an 'invisible hand' by providing back-end funding and advisory services rather than just financing the equipment.

A few months later, Srei partnered with Tata Iron and Steel Company (TISCO) on a chromite mine project and financed an excavator for G.S. Atwal and Company.
WB 496

Asset-backed leasing became a niche for Srei.
Thanks Sunil; who else could we have gone to other than Srei when we needed asset financing? You have made a very good name for yourselves in the market.
We are all contributing to the growth of India's infrastructure. Srei's doing its bit.

W B·496
The zeal to excel in this domain grew stronger as India initiated economic reforms in the 1990s, leading to the growth of the leasing sector and also enhancing the scope of private participation in the development of its infrastructure.

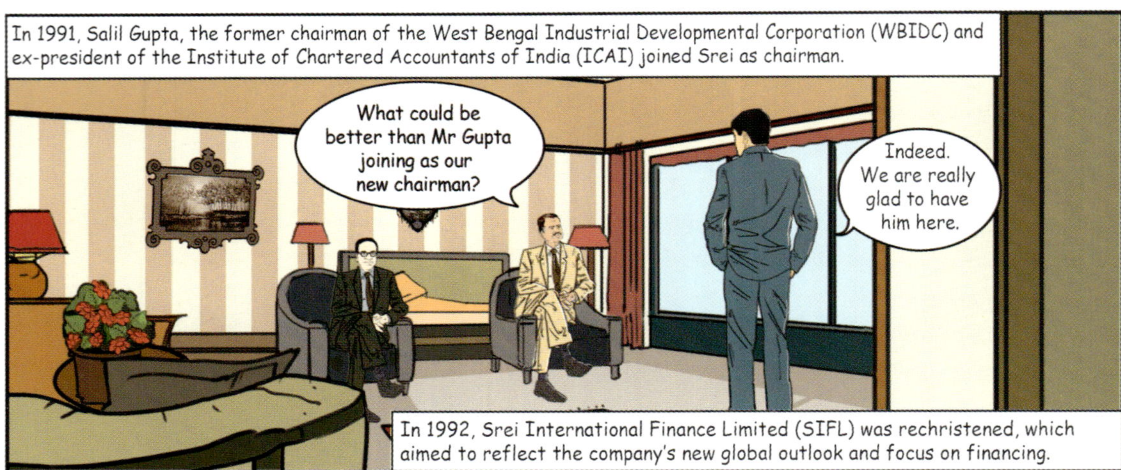
In 1991, Salil Gupta, the former chairman of the West Bengal Industrial Developmental Corporation (WBIDC) and ex-president of the Institute of Chartered Accountants of India (ICAI) joined Srei as chairman.
What could be better than Mr Gupta joining as our new chairman?
Indeed. We are really glad to have him here.
In 1992, Srei International Finance Limited (SIFL) was rechristened, which aimed to reflect the company's new global outlook and focus on financing.

The Kanorias decided that it was the right time to go public. Hence, SIFL issued an Initial Public Offer (IPO) of Rs 2.24 crore on 3 May 1992.

On the morning of the launch, after their customary round of squash and tennis at the club...
It's a fortunate day!
To reach on time, we need to start early. There will be heavy traffic at this hour.
WB 0328
But destiny had other plans...

A speeding bus collided with their car as they were driving through the National Library crossing. It happened so quickly that Hemant could not divert the car. Before they knew it, the bus had done the damage.

Hemant and Sunil were severely injured, but somehow Hemant drove to a nearby hospital.

Both were taken to the intensive care unit...

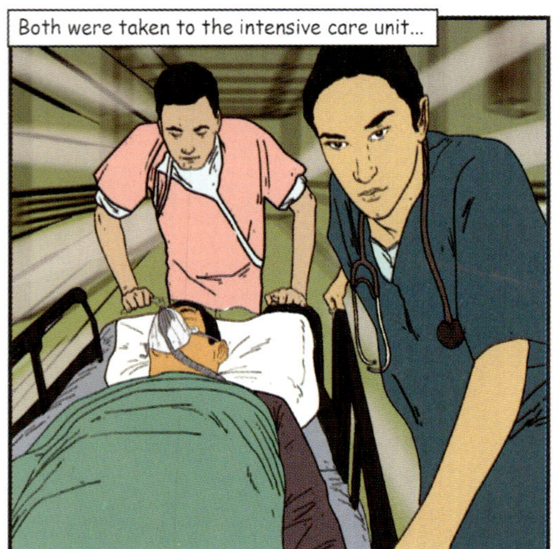

Their neighbour, Dr Banerjee, rushed to the hospital to help upon hearing the news.

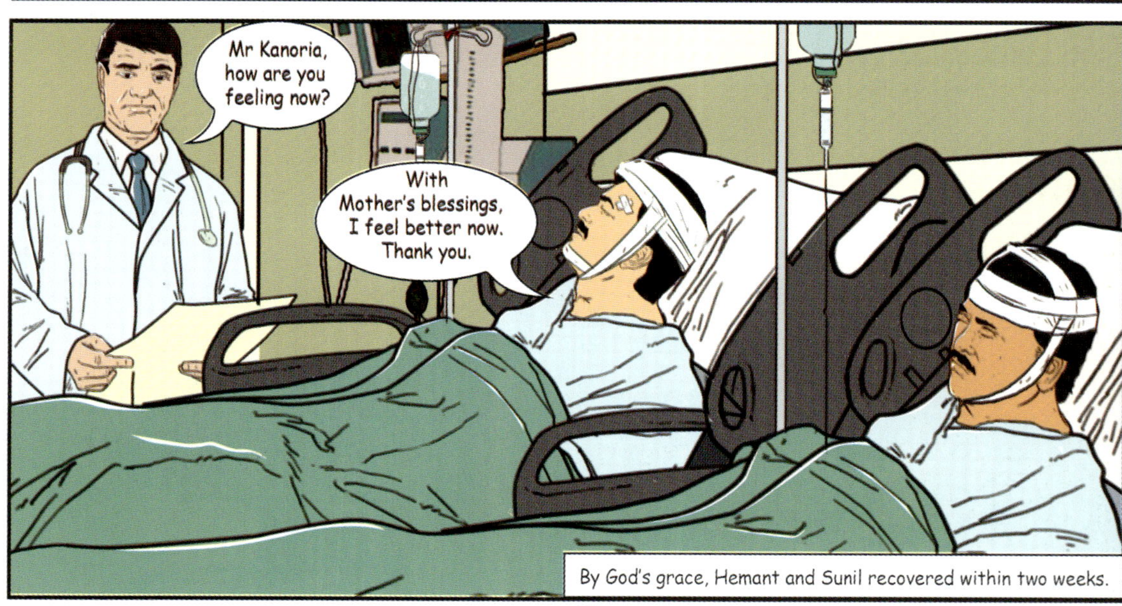

By God's grace, Hemant and Sunil recovered within two weeks.

Hemant was back to work immediately upon recovery, against the doctor's advice.
Hemant, what are you doing here in office, you should be at home, shouldn't you? You should take care of your health above all else.
Father, I feel much better. You need not worry.

Minutes later, Mr Gupta's face lit up as he walked into Hemant's chamber.
Ah! Good to see you back, Hemant.

It feels good to be back!

Emerging stronger after the incident, the brothers were successful in taking Srei public...
IPO
launc
srei
srei
IPO
launch
CLAP!!
CLAP!!
CLAP!!
CLAP!!
...and conducted the IPO promotions in the country throughout the next year. They were ready to explore new horizons.

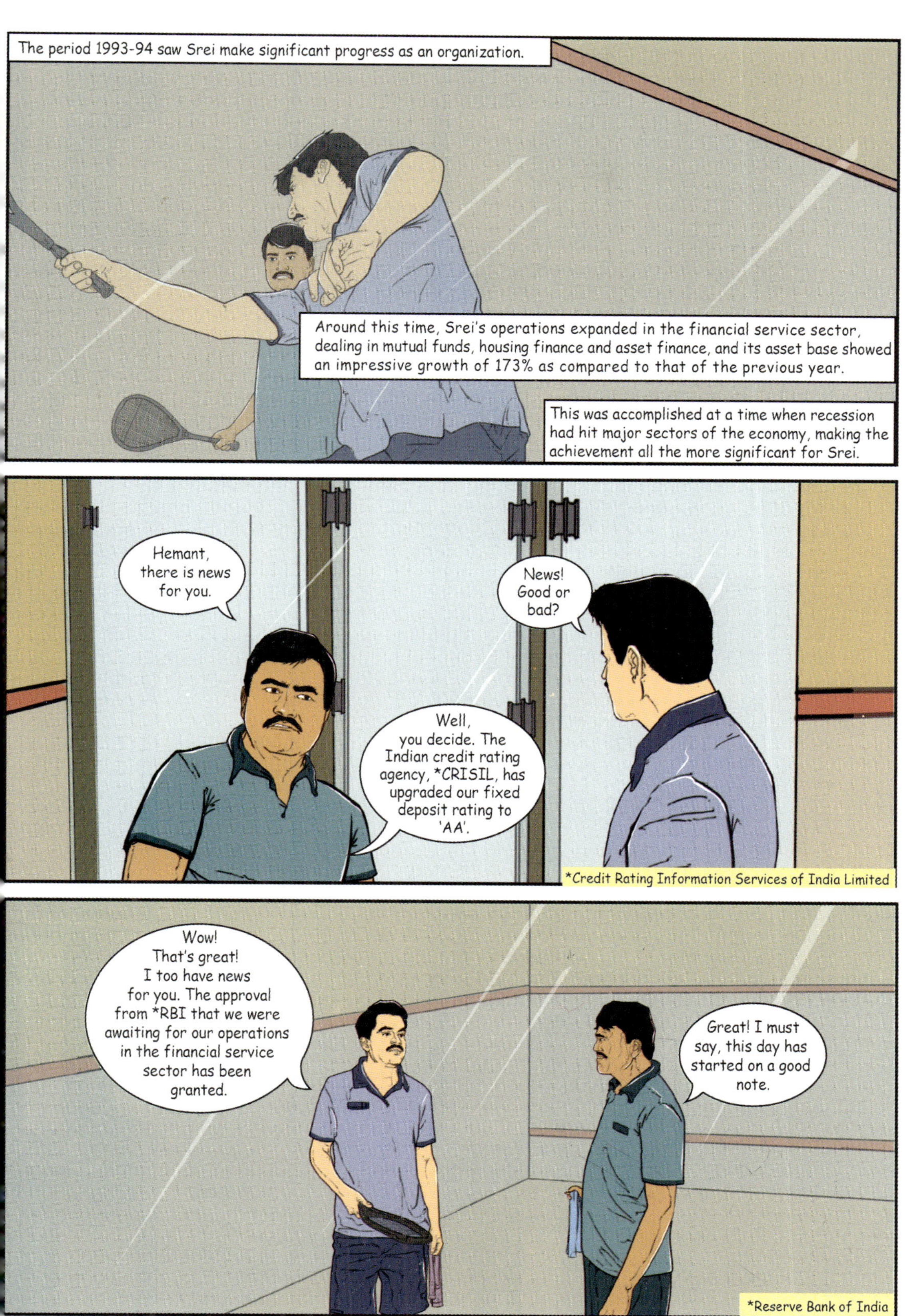
The period 1993-94 saw Srei make significant progress as an organization.
Around this time, Srei's operations expanded in the financial service sector, dealing in mutual funds, housing finance and asset finance, and its asset base showed an impressive growth of 173% as compared to that of the previous year.
This was accomplished at a time when recession had hit major sectors of the economy, making the achievement all the more significant for Srei.
Hemant, there is news for you.
News! Good or bad?
Well, you decide. The Indian credit rating agency, *CRISIL, has upgraded our fixed deposit rating to 'AA'.
*Credit Rating Information Services of India Limited
Wow! That's great! I too have news for you. The approval from *RBI that we were awaiting for our operations in the financial service sector has been granted.
Great! I must say, this day has started on a good note.
*Reserve Bank of India

Later that day...
Sir, a gentleman from L&T is here.
Oh. he is here already. Please send him in.

Mr Kanoria, there is an urgent requirement for excavators at a railway site in Barbil.
In that case, it's best we travel to Barbil tomorrow.

Next day...
JK TYRE
See, Mr Kanoria, these contractors are ill-equipped...
OR-02 F-4432

The banks ask for too many documents that these people can't put together.

Throughout their journey, Mr Bhattacharya gave Sunil all the necessary information regarding the project.
We have almost reached...another five minutes...

At the site, the project manager, Mr Jhawar, looked worried.
Mr Kanoria, as I told you, this costs about Rs 20 lakh.
I need to load the iron ore into these railway wagons. This job requires about 500 workers and 22-25 days, however, an excavator can do it in just five days.
BARBIL

We are not concerned about his performance in the last financial year if the present one is in order.

Also, it's important to know how much he is capable of paying.
He is capable of paying around Rs 8 lakh. But the asset costs Rs 20 lakh.

We can provide him the asset. I've told him that we do not give cash loans because only commercial banks function that way.

Good, we will give him the excavator so that it remains our asset.

In that case, we must go ahead.
Sure, have a word with him regarding this. Have a good day, Sunil!

Congratulations Mr Jhawar, your excavator will be with you very soon. My team will get in touch with you and explain the necessary steps to be taken, along with the terms and conditions of the contract.
Thank you, Mr Kanoria...That will be a great help.

Meanwhile, in Srei's office...
Yes, Mr Dutta... Not a problem! Tomorrow will be fine... Yes, I know about the political turmoil in Assam...

Next day, in Sibsagar, Assam, Sunil drove past petroleum drilling rigs. With him was Asim Dutta from Tractors India Limited (TIL), an equipment manufacturing company in Kolkata.
Mr Kanoria, the contractor requires a crane for a petroleum barrage being built for *ONGC.
*Oil and Natural Gas Corporation

An hour later, over tea at a local café...
I propose that my company, TIL, gives the contractor the crane and you provide the cash. The cash flow will improve that way.

But, Mr Dutta, we do not give loans; we lend assets.

Oh yes! How could I forget? Thanks for correcting me.

Later that day, Sunil had a meeting with the contractor at his office.
Thank you for meeting me. Banks have refused to help me because I don't have a proper balance sheet. Will Srei do the same?

No, if you have a proper cash flow statement that meets our requirement, we'll provide you with the crane. That too, in a very short time.

Great! I'll provide you the necessary statements.
Please do. I'll go through them myself and my team will get back to you.

Thank you, Mr Kanoria, Srei has come to my rescue when the banks were unwilling.
You are welcome, Mr Jain. We are helping you because we believe in you.

Around this time, Srei laid considerable emphasis on the quality of assets that it was lending.

While maintaining a diversified portfolio and financing big-ticket leasing, the organization ensured a very close liaison with individual clients while monitoring their business activities.
Srei always maintained an effective system of recovery and reoccupying of equipment...

The company was successful in maintaining a zero-debt position along with a decent recovery rate.

Working closely with customers allowed Srei management to learn about project life-cycle complexities.

This provided the organization with valuable insight regarding the key attributes of various project life cycles and about their working capital needs.
Now, Srei was well on its way to becoming a leader in project financing.

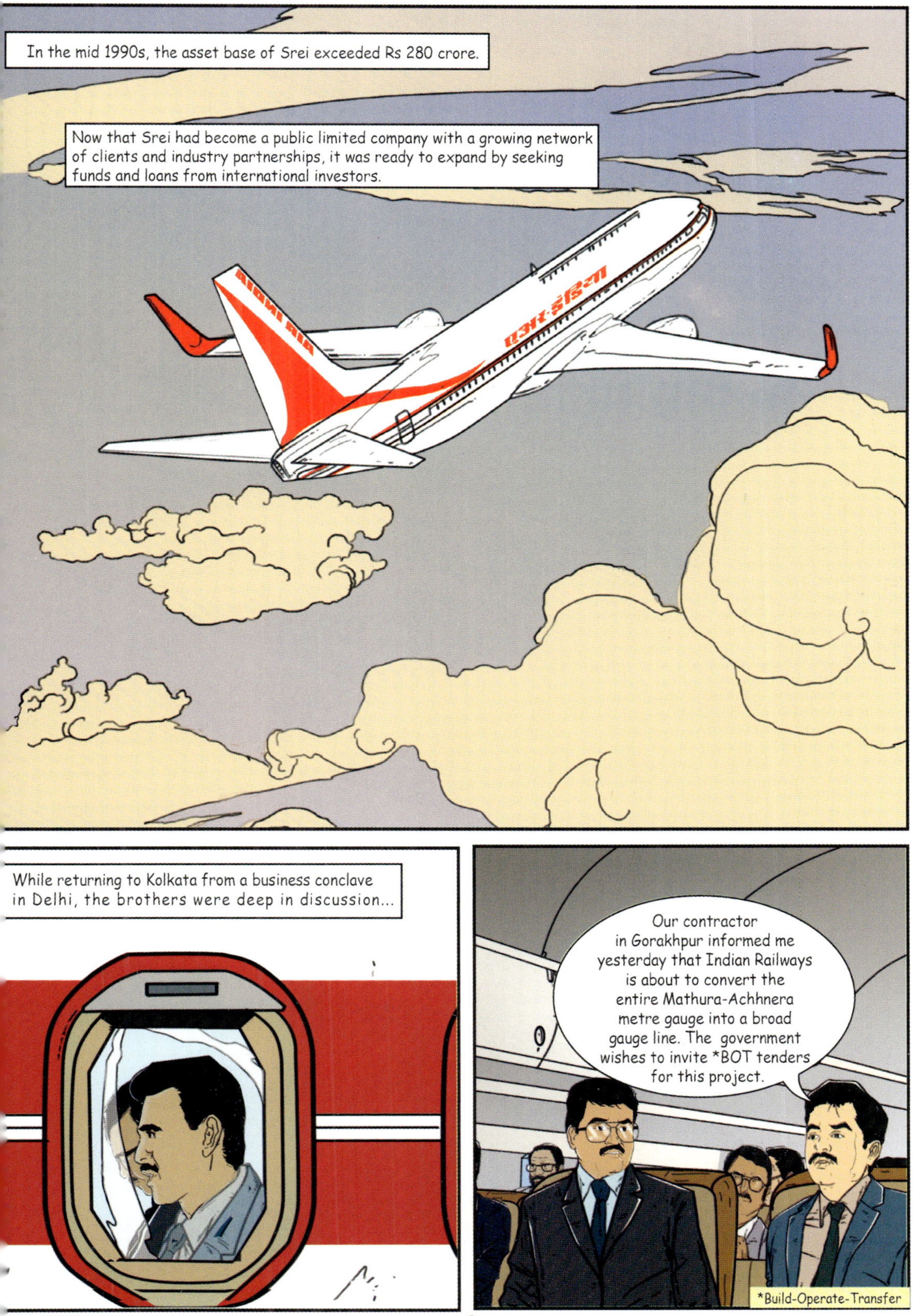

In the mid 1990s, the asset base of Srei exceeded Rs 280 crore.

Now that Srei had become a public limited company with a growing network of clients and industry partnerships, it was ready to expand by seeking funds and loans from international investors.

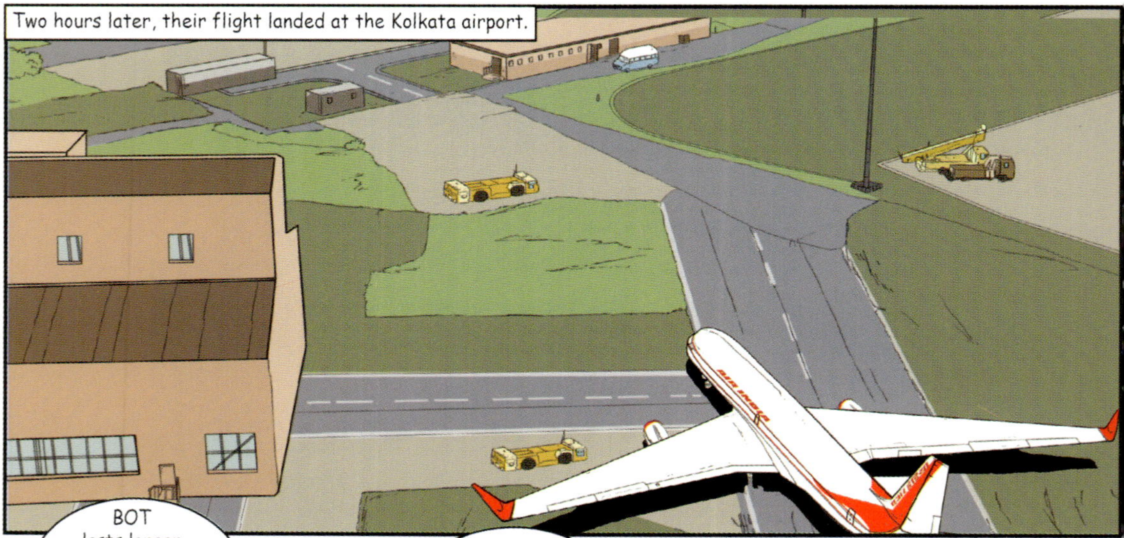

Two hours later, their flight landed at the Kolkata airport.

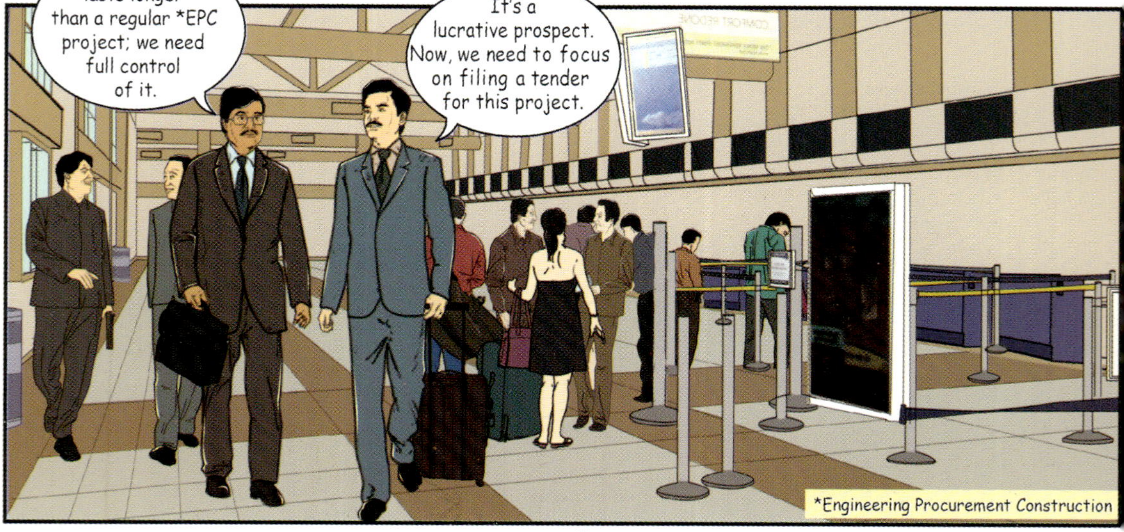

BOT lasts longer than a regular *EPC project; we need full control of it.

It's a lucrative prospect. Now, we need to focus on filing a tender for this project.

*Engineering Procurement Construction

The bidding process was completed by the brothers within the next few days.
Well, we have done the best we could... Now, it is up to fate.
Hmm... By the way there is news... The Dalal Street Journal has rated Srei as the eighth best finance company in India.
That's fantastic! We have done pretty well, I must say!

At the 1996 annual gala dinner at the Bengal Chamber of Commerce and Industry (BCC&I) headquarters in Calcutta...
...Hemant got a call from his office.

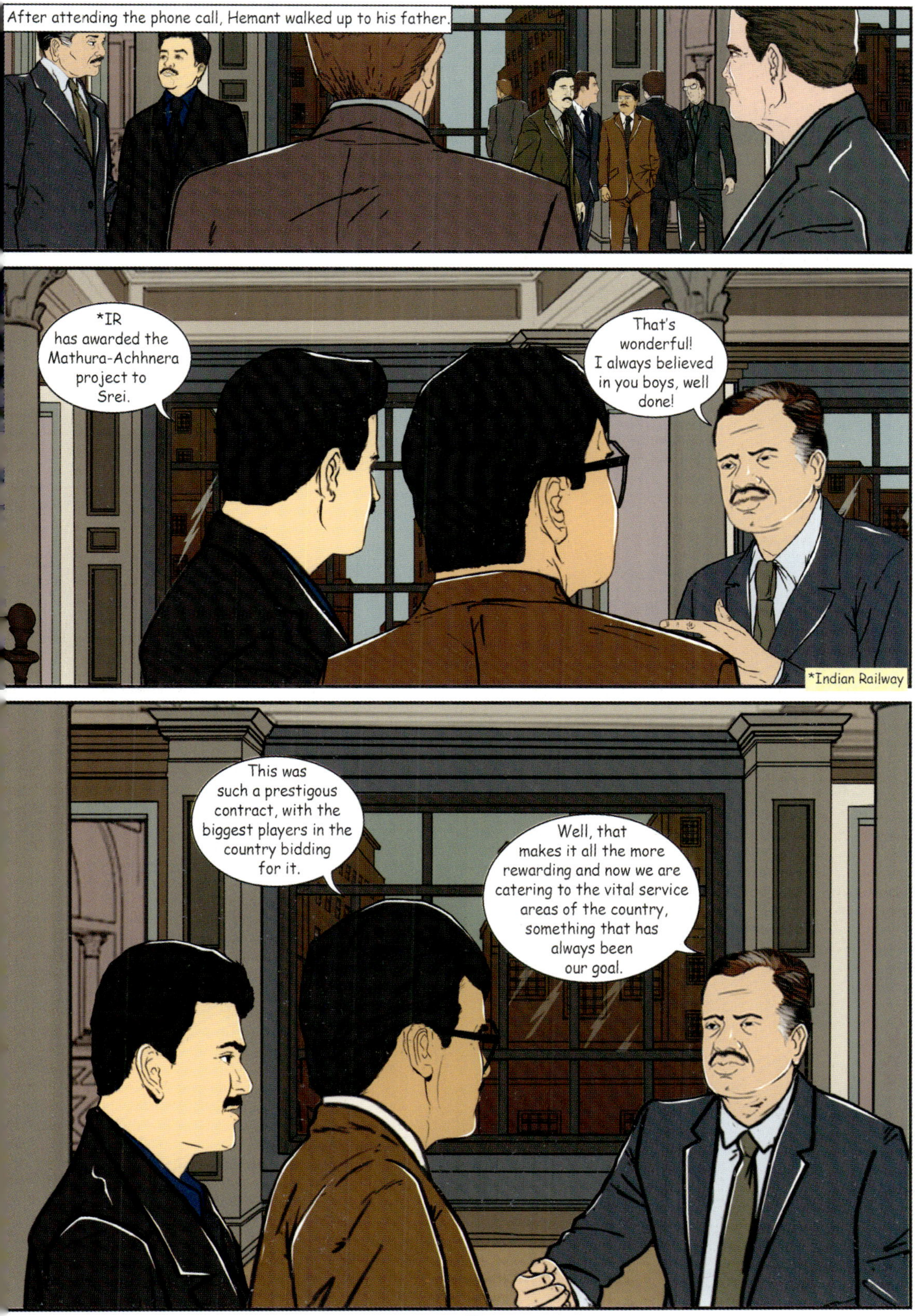

This was such a prestigous contract, with the biggest players in the country bidding for it.

Well, that makes it all the more rewarding and now we are catering to the vital service areas of the country, something that has always been our goal.

Next day...
RING RING
Hello... Yes, good morning, Alice.
Sir, Mr Klaus Benz of *DEG Germany called. He met you at the Bengal Club at an Indo-German Chamber of Commerce meeting.
*Deutsche Investitions- und Entwicklungsgesellschaft
Thanks, Alice. Please send me his contact details.
Later...
Hello, Mr Benz, good morning. This is Sunil Kanoria from Srei...
Hello Sunil, I'm keen to meet you. Your office informed me that you might be flying to Germany next week; we could meet at my office.
Yes... That won't be a problem, I am landing on the 17th. Have a good day.

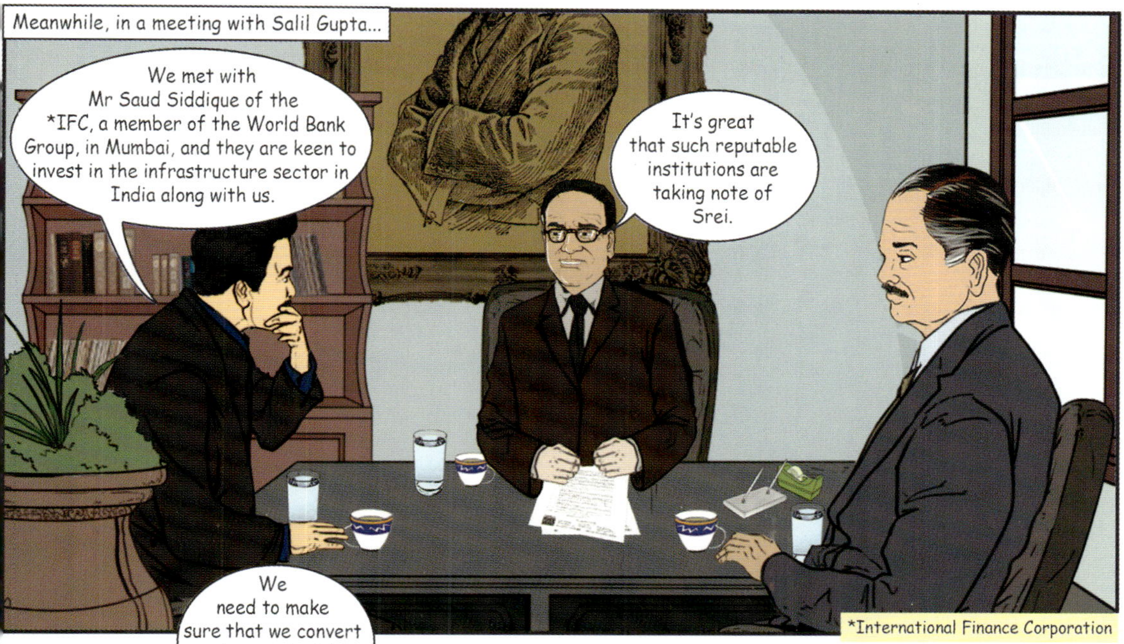

Meanwhile, in a meeting with Salil Gupta...

We met with Mr Saud Siddique of the *IFC, a member of the World Bank Group, in Mumbai, and they are keen to invest in the infrastructure sector in India along with us.

It's great that such reputable institutions are taking note of Srei.

*International Finance Corporation

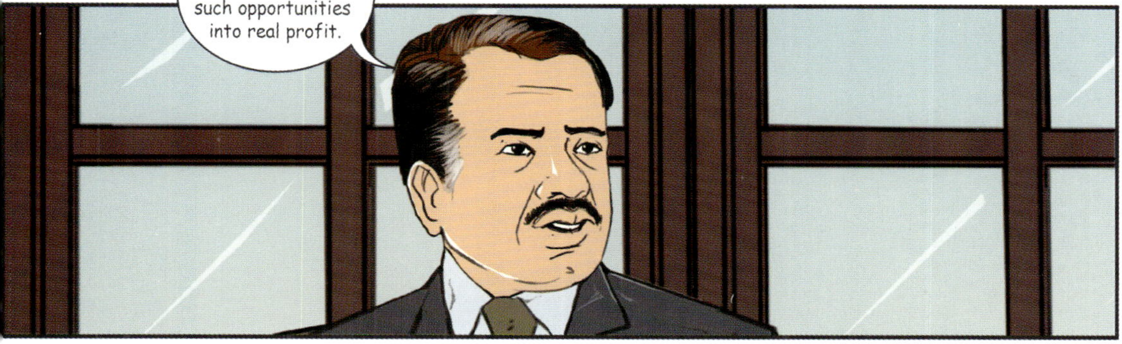

We need to make sure that we convert such opportunities into real profit.

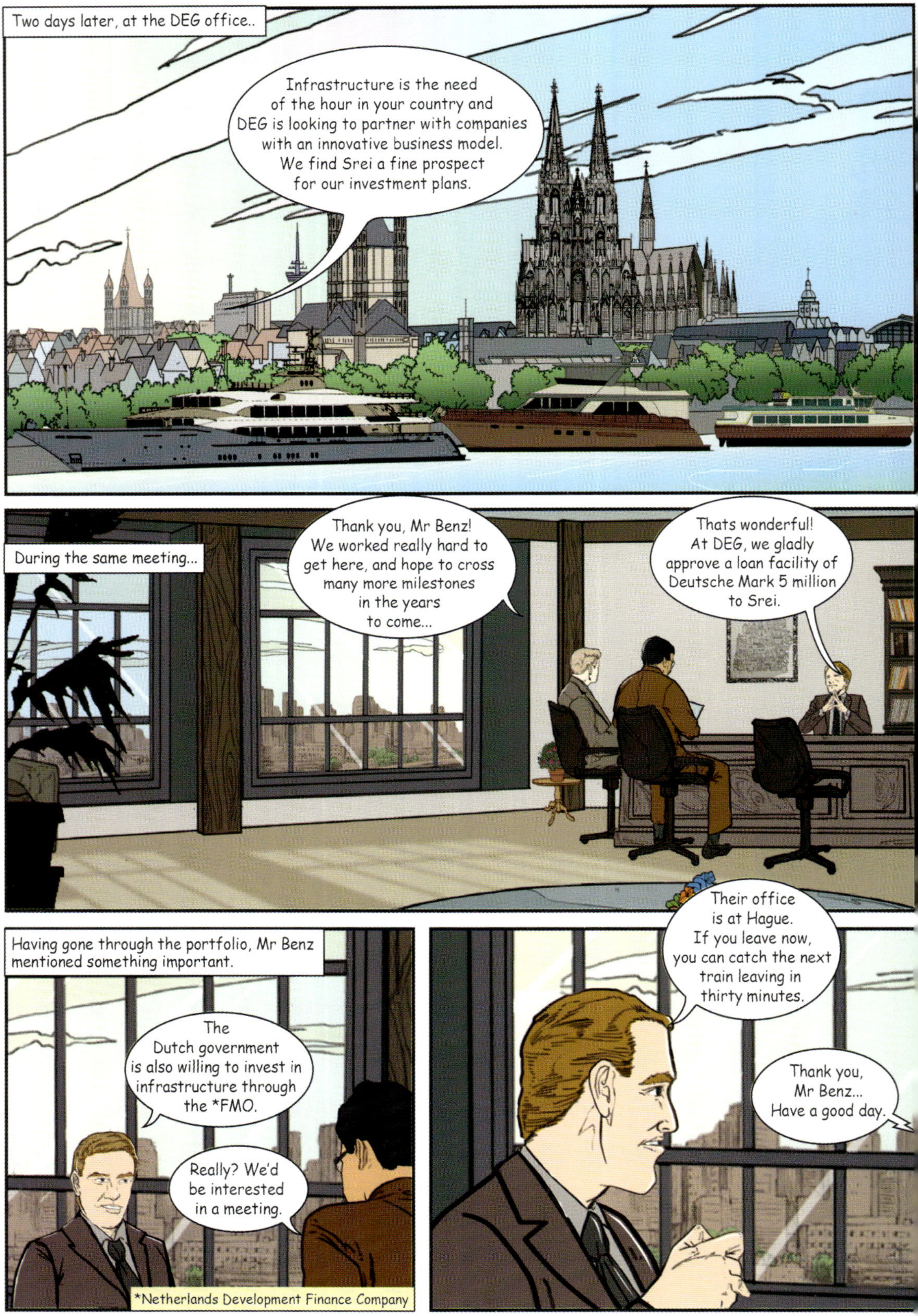

During the same meeting...

Thank you, Mr Benz! We worked really hard to get here, and hope to cross many more milestones in the years to come...

Thats wonderful! At DEG, we gladly approve a loan facility of Deutsche Mark 5 million to Srei.

Having gone through the portfolio, Mr Benz mentioned something important.

The Dutch government is also willing to invest in infrastructure through the *FMO.

Really? We'd be interested in a meeting.

*Netherlands Development Finance Company

Their office is at Hague. If you leave now, you can catch the next train leaving in thirty minutes.

Thank you, Mr Benz... Have a good day.

Taxi!
Railway station, please!
TAXI

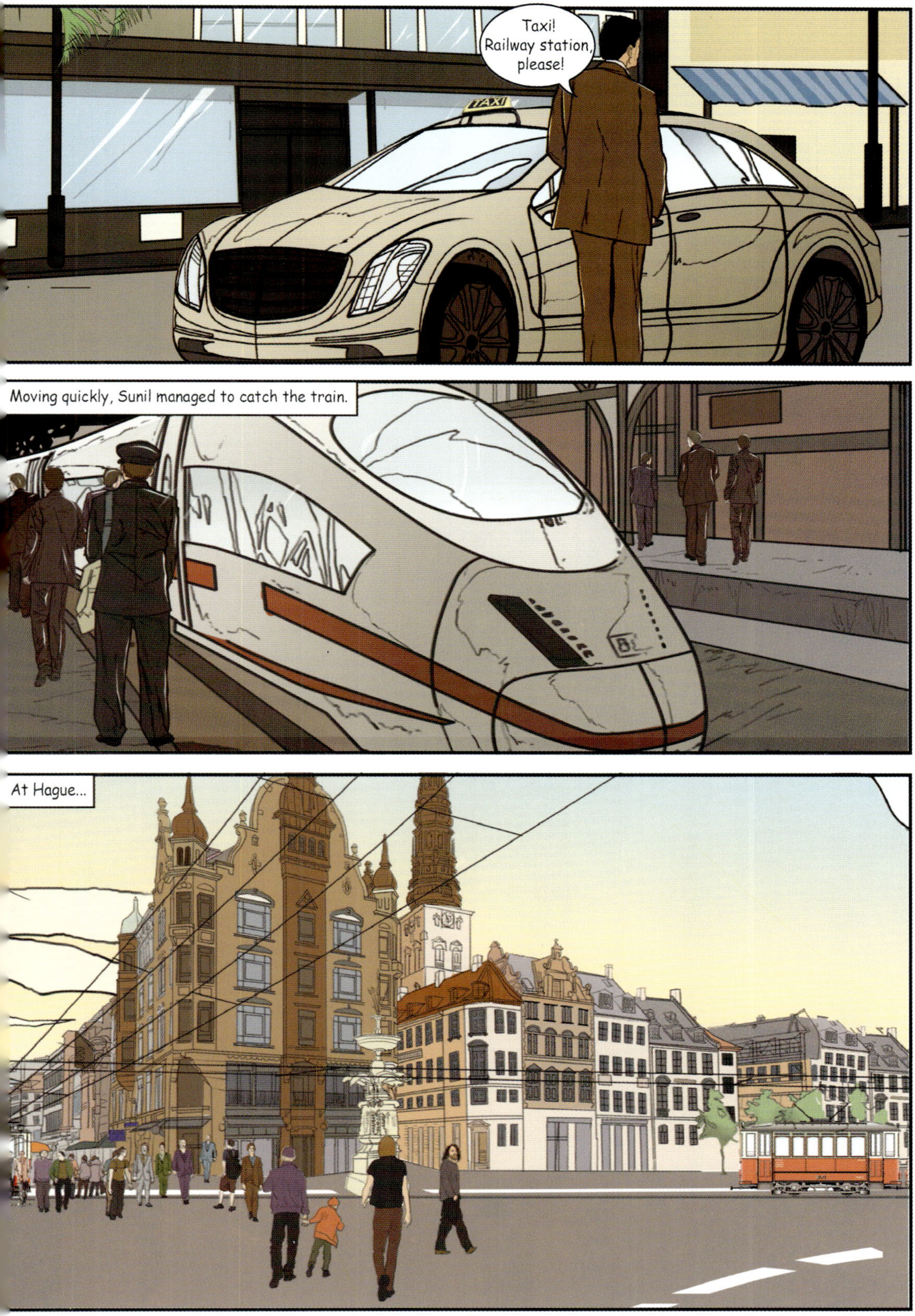

Moving quickly, Sunil managed to catch the train.

At Hague...

At the FMO...
Sir, do you have an appointment?
Yes, Ma'am...

Sunil met Geritt van Kampen, senior executive at the FMO and made a presentation.

A fine presentation Mr Kanoria, and so is your profile. I will forward these documents to my seniors.
Thank you.
srei

Meanwhile, in India...
Sunil, Business India has nominated Srei as a contender for the Super 100 finance companies. Yes...yes...I am fine; you too, take care.

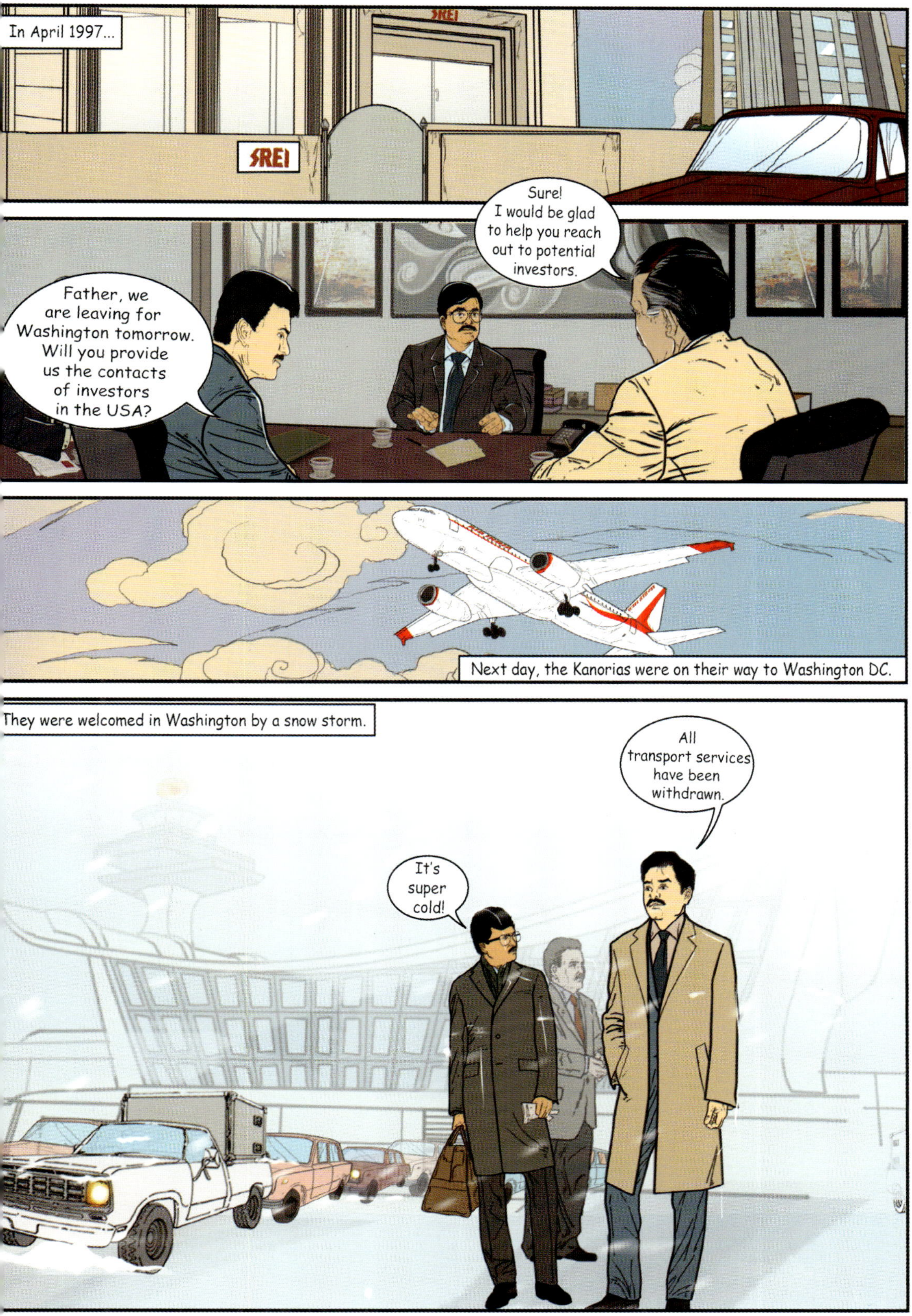

They were welcomed in Washington by a snow storm.

All transport services have been withdrawn.

It's super cold!

Later...
Sunil, I just spoke with Mr Siddique's assistant, he will meet us the day after tomorrow.

We need to make room to meet with a few area experts as well, to learn about best practices.
Well, our itinerary is filling up with meetings very quickly.

Braving the rough weather of Washington, Hemant and Sunil attended a series of meetings...

At a renowned financial consultancy firm...
Since last year, our asset base has increased 173% year-on-year.

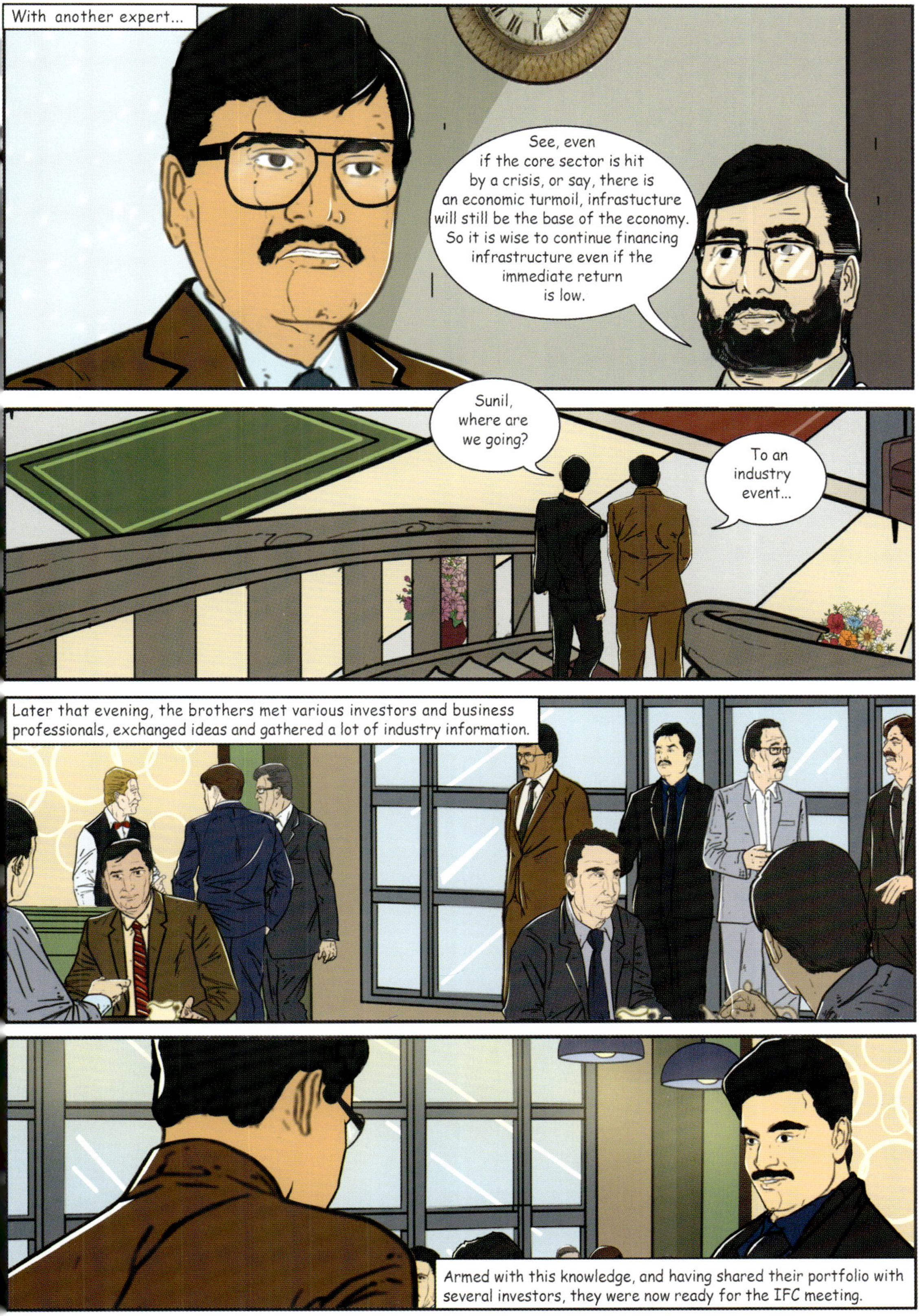

With another expert...

See, even if the core sector is hit by a crisis, or say, there is an economic turmoil, infrastucture will still be the base of the economy. So it is wise to continue financing infrastructure even if the immediate return is low.

Sunil, where are we going?

To an industry event...

Meanwhile in India, news of a serious stock market scam unfolded, as Salil Gupta and Hari Prasad Kanoria watched...
This is disgraceful! The scam has become an international shame within hours.
Resorting to the oldest and I must say the cheapest trick: manipulating the stock market for personal gain... Shameful!

This stain on *NBFCs will discourage investors. That's bad for us, isn't it?
It's a real shame, I admit, but Srei operates with integrity and honesty. We will set a good example.
*Non-Banking Financial Company

But developing our institutions to offer security to the market will take time. Are there mature enough players to prove integrity to investors?
Well, I am very sure that with Srei's strong performance, we can restore investors' confidence in India's infrastructure sector.

Back in Washington in a meeting at the IFC...
I have gone through Srei's profile. From leasing to project appraisal, from loan syndication to fund placement, you have covered a lot of ground in a very short time.
When foreign institutions like the IFC show faith in our ideas, we believe that we will be able to do better to support India's economic growth.
Well, I am certain that infrastructure in India will improve within a very short time and PPP will become increasingly relevant in the near future.
There is a lot of scope but it needs investment and restructuring of government policies.
As I said, I am personally very impressed with Srei's performance over the last five years. However, I do have a small concern...

What is your concern, Mr Siddique?

The current size of your initiative might come across as a bit too limited for the IFC.

Mr Siddique, I believe that the IFC, in all its wisdom, will go by our ability, not by the size.
Let's hope so. I will get in touch with you once I have had a meeting with the board.

Back in India, in the late 1990s, the government was trying to ease the infrastructure bottleneck and increase private participation, but the Indian economy was repeatedly hit by a number of scams.

In Kolkata, Hemant and Sunil were in conversation with a banker friend.
These scams have shaken the faith of investors in NBFCs.
Exactly! It is making things all the more difficult in the absence of regulations in this regard.

Our recovery rate has considerably dropped ever since this has happened. We need to figure out a solution to this problem.

The brothers and the management team conferred on how to handle the situation and they came up with a plan.
Hemant, I have observed that the performance of the debt market was quite impressive last year. If that is repeated, there will be certain debt issues in the market.
Yes, I too was thinking that to safeguard ourselves from this crisis, we must focus on debt instruments for our clients.

Problems compounded for the NBFCs as the Reserve Bank of India (RBI) came out with new guidelines, which stated that the NBFCs could not mobilize deposits and banks could not lend money. The Kanoria brothers now approached the UnitTrust of India (UTI).
UNIT TRUST OF INDIA

We will issue compulsorily convertible preference shares. The instrument has been rated AAA(*SO) and there is no risk involved for the buyer. This is a unique debt instrument.
TRUST OF INDIA
*Statutory Obligation

You see, when the instrument is converted, the investor becomes a shareholder of the company.

Sounds good! Can you tell me the monetary value of this issue?
It's worth Rs 100 crore for the time being. We will gauge its acceptance by the stakeholders and adjust accordingly.

The brothers promoted this issue to other financial institutions. They also felt that the knowledge they had gathered about investment in infrastructure from their foreign tours could be utilized at this point...

They decided to diversify, despite the low profit margins, with the vision that infrastructure equipment would never lose its relevance as development of infrastructure was a continuous process.
Here is the list of assets having a life span of more than ten years. These have significant resale value.

As the UTI along with other institutions decided to invest in its debentures, Srei had its presence in fifteen cities in India...

...focusing on steady and continuous growth, and more importantly, keeping the safety of their investors as top priority.

Around this time, in 1997, Srei filed a tender with a reputable state-owned power company to finance a 25 MW power project in Odisha.
Srei seems to have a clear idea on this matter. It is among the few private financers of infrastructure-related equipment in India and I think it is ready to venture into other domains.

The officials of the state ministry looked through the proposal more meticulously in the days that followed.

Later...
Thank you, sir, this will help us cater to the state's power needs more effectively.

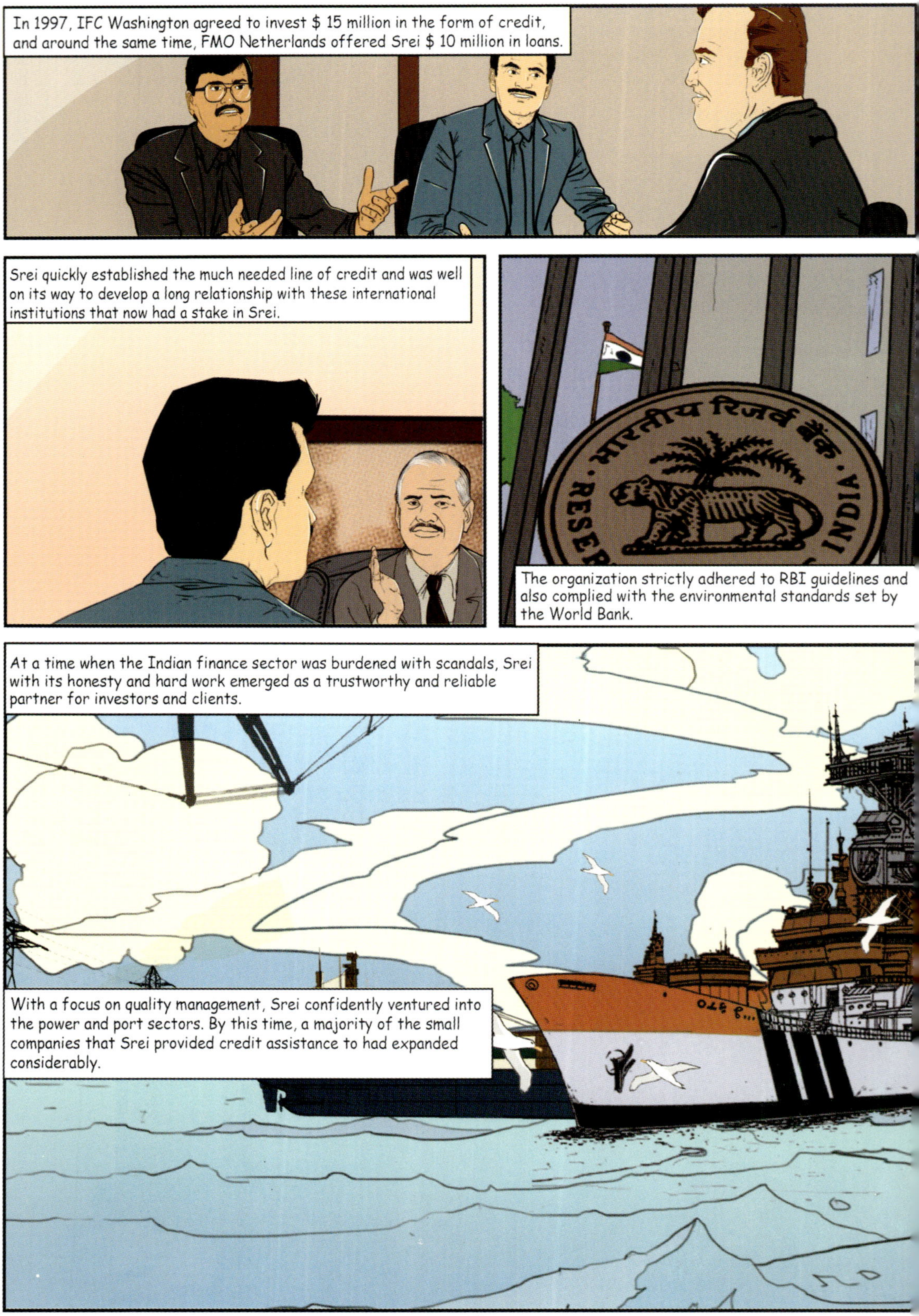

Srei quickly established the much needed line of credit and was well on its way to develop a long relationship with these international institutions that now had a stake in Srei.

At a time when the Indian finance sector was burdened with scandals, Srei with its honesty and hard work emerged as a trustworthy and reliable partner for investors and clients.

With a focus on quality management, Srei confidently ventured into the power and port sectors. By this time, a majority of the small companies that Srei provided credit assistance to had expanded considerably.

Srei was increasingly becoming known for its contributions to help the economy develop and grow, but now it was time for the company to hire more qualified talent.

At the Kanoria residence...
We want people from the industry with a strong financial background and the ability to contribute to our funding needs.

And we need experts in credit assessment and risk management.

Later...
Based on our discussion, I have made a list comprising the characteristics we would be looking for in our prospective recruits.
Let me have a look.

The brothers discussed the same with their father the next day over breakfast.
We plan to build our management team with people who have substantial banking experience and good entrepreneurial skills. What do you think?
Sounds promising! Along with entrepreneurial skills, let us also emphasize the need for candidates to develop existing strategies and expand projects.

A few days later, Srei placed job announcements in the papers.
The Statesman
'Looking to hire a range of mid- and senior-level professionals with experience in industry and business analysis, finance, and project management for Srei, a growing infrastructure finance company. Interested candidates may apply.'

The Kanorias began interviewing short-listed candidates after careful analysis of numerous resumes.

A few hours later, in the interview room...
Yet to find the right candidate, after all these interviews.
Didn't realize it would be this difficult!

After several interviews...
KNOCK
Hello... May I come in?
KNOCK

The visitor was D.K. Vyas, who had been associated with Srei as an auditor for G.P. Agarwal in Delhi.
Good afternoon, thank you for calling me for this interview.
Good afternoon, Mr Vyas, please have a seat.

We are impressed with your experience and accomplishments.

Mr Vyas, what, according to you, are the steps that must be taken by Srei in order to grow in the area of infrastructure financing?
I would suggest you continue to focus on asset financing but keep in mind the future of project financing and how you can prepare for changes in the market.
Doing so would help you retain your stronghold on what you are currently doing, while also preparing for diversification since many segments are yet to be tapped by the private sector.
I see... What other advice do you have for us?
Perhaps diversify your service model to create a value chain for both your assets and customers. You would then work towards securing your returns and maintaining and managing assets, so as to assure a regular and strong cash flow.
Thank you Mr Vyas, we will be in touch.

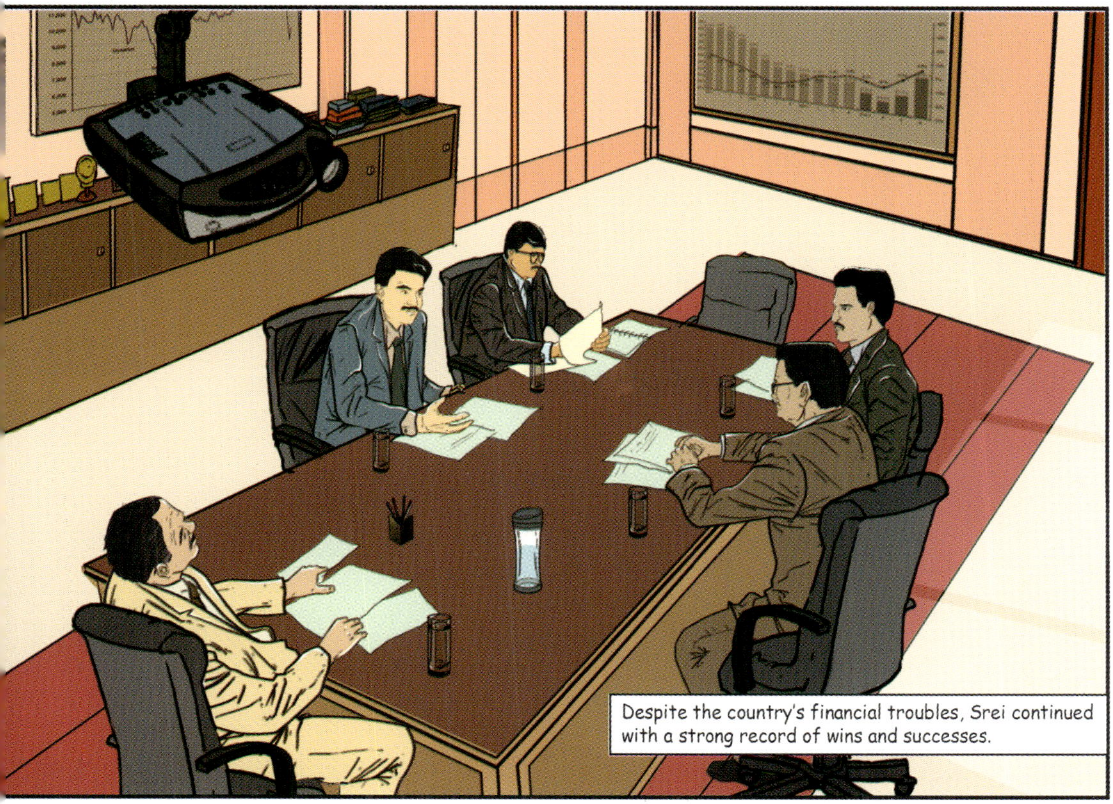

Despite the country's financial troubles, Srei continued with a strong record of wins and successes.

As the 1990s drew to a close and the new millennium began, Srei ventured into a new domain with Srei Renewable Energy Unit (Sreu).
Congratulations on the launch of Sreu.
Thank you. We promote environment-friendly infrastructure development in villages.
Later...
After our research on renewable energy and discussions with the *IREDA, we can now go ahead with our initiative.
Yes, I am certain that our collaboration with the IFC and the World Bank is a step in the right direction.
*Indian Renewable Energy Development Agency Ltd.
Srei launched a six-year project with the IFC worth Rs 65 crore to develop solar energy systems in rural India.
The project was implemented on behalf of the World Bank's global environmental facility.
Srei helped install 850 home lighting systems in rural West Bengal, particularly the Sundarbans, and 450 lighting systems and 1,200 solar lanterns in Leh, Ladakh, Kargil and other remote areas.
Srei also distributed 400 solar water pumps in Punjab, Tamil Nadu, Karnataka, West Bengal and Maharashtra, as well as 675 solar water heaters to Bharat Heavy Electricals Limited (BHEL), in Bhopal, Secunderabad and Ranipet.

Srei's next move was to establish a partnership with the Dishergarh Power Supply Corporation (DPSC).
Mr Kanoria, the DPSC needs to boost generation by setting up a 10 MW capacity unit.
Okay, we think, we can help you with that.
*Dishergarh Power Supply Corporation

In parallel, the company financed its first barge power plant in Karnataka.

Simultaneously, another important step was being taken...
We will be entering investment banking with Srei Capital Markets Ltd., taking up infrastructure development assignments and collaborating with various government and private organizations. We need to focus on all this.

However, all was not well on the global front. On 11 September 2001, the world was rocked by a massive terror attack on New York's World Trade Centre.
This tragic event not only claimed lives, but it triggered panic throughout the international financial markets.
Srei at this point decided to secure assets and long-term loans from the market to insulate itself from the economic crisis generated by this tragedy.
SREI
ISSUE MANAGEMENT
LOAN SYNDICATION
FUND PLACEMENT
INVESTMENT BANKING
CORPORATE ADVISORY SERVICES
LEASING AND HIRE PURCHASE
INTER-CORPORATE DEPOSITS
PROJECT APPRAISALS
Indeed, during this time, Srei's non-performing assets dropped from 1.74% to 1.32%, one of the best standards ever achieved by a financial organization in India.
In 2001, Srei raised unsecured subordinated bonds in the nature of mezzanine capital, the project they had earlier discussed with the UTI and other investors.
Hemant, our issue of mezzanine capital has raised Rs 52 crore.
That's great. We are the first company in India to issue mezzanine in the market. I am sure, others will follow.

In 2002, Srei reached a new milestone in the area of infrastructure project financing.
The *NH 5 and NH 9 are extremely important for the development of Andhra Pradesh. On behalf of the government, I wish Srei the very best.
Sir, it's an honour to be part of this project.
*National Highway
Next day at the office...
From what I gather from the reports shared by Mr Vyas today, it's the largest BOT project in India till date.
True, after our success with NH 6 in Maharashtra, I am sure, we will be a step ahead in aiding the development of NH 5 and NH 9.
The conversation continued as the Kanorias headed for the airport to catch a flight to Delhi.
The national importance of the projects we are involved in, will give us an edge in the future. We should never break this momentum.
Sure, and making things even better is 100% *FDI provision from the government.
*Foreign Direct Investment

However, India's growing automobile industry continued to exert immense pressure on the country's road networks.

As passenger and heavy vehicles became more affordable, their numbers grew exponentially...
V.Logistics

The government struggled to develop networks to accommodate the increasing freight traffic...
LADAKH
...specially in India's hinterlands.

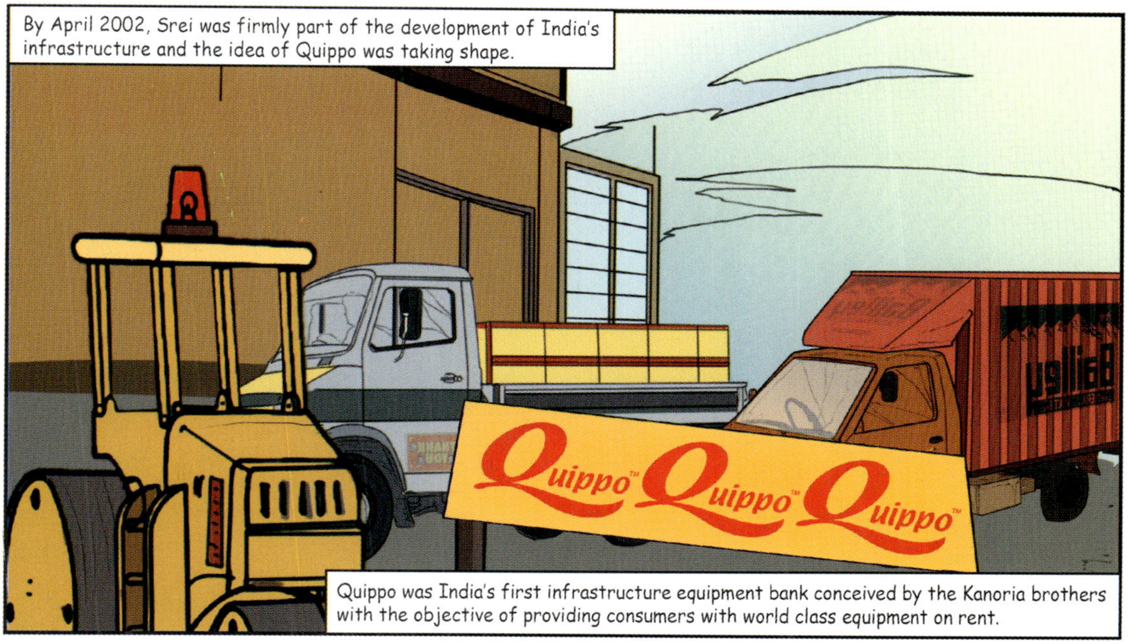

By April 2002, Srei was firmly part of the development of India's infrastructure and the idea of Quippo was taking shape.

Quippo was India's first infrastructure equipment bank conceived by the Kanoria brothers with the objective of providing consumers with world class equipment on rent.

However, Sunil had a wider vision for Quippo...
I have been researching on sectors like energy, oil, gas and telecom. These are rapidly expanding and we can include these sectors under the brand.

I'm particularly keen on exploring the telecom tower business.
Hmm... Sounds good, given that telecom is growing at a decent pace. Let's start working on it!

A month later, with Sunil as the driving force, Quippo entered the telecom and energy rental sector.
Quippo™
Quippo Telecom Infrastructure Ltd

In 2003-04, Srei disbursed Rs 63 crore in the power, railway and port sectors.
Also to Srei's credit were two landmark infrastructure projects in Afghanistan.
Other notable projects during this time included the Delhi-Gurgaon highway, the Swarna toll way and two state highways in Madhya Pradesh. As far as organized growth was concerned, Srei had branches in thirty cities across India. The company leased 400 solar pumps in Punjab, Tamil Nadu, Karnataka and West Bengal.
This is an old map; not to scale.

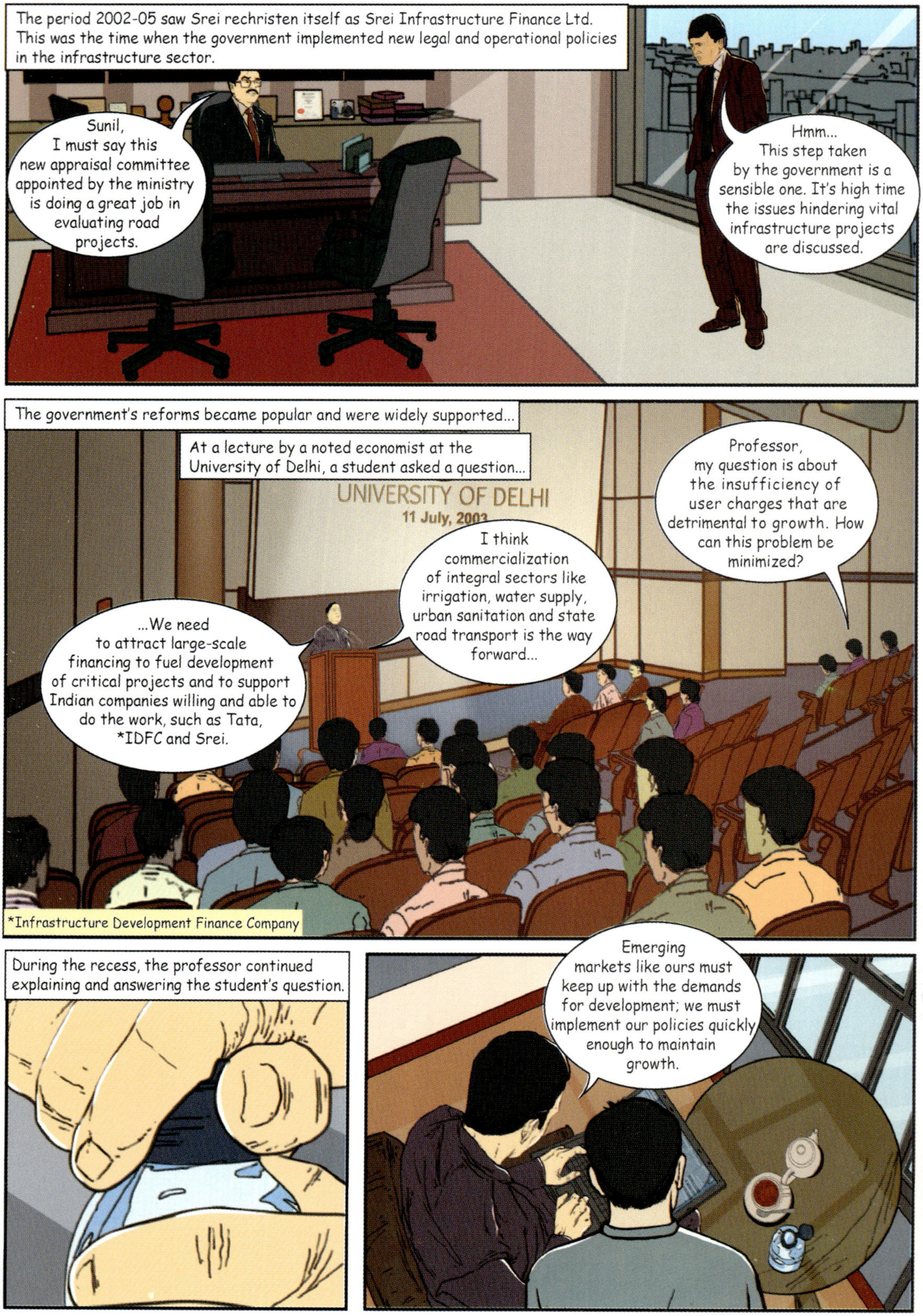

The government's reforms became popular and were widely supported...

At a lecture by a noted economist at the University of Delhi, a student asked a question...

UNIVERSITY OF DELHI
11 July, 2003

Professor, my question is about the insufficiency of user charges that are detrimental to growth. How can this problem be minimized?

I think commercialization of integral sectors like irrigation, water supply, urban sanitation and state road transport is the way forward...

...We need to attract large-scale financing to fuel development of critical projects and to support Indian companies willing and able to do the work, such as Tata, *IDFC and Srei.

*Infrastructure Development Finance Company

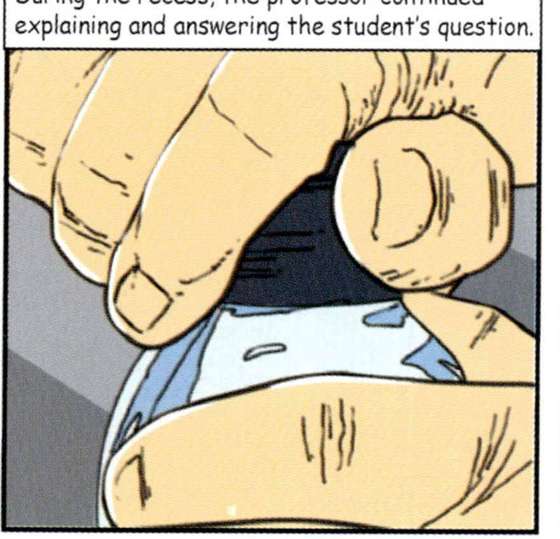

Even noted economists and scholars of the country had started considering Srei as one of the top players in the construction equipment financing segment.
Srei was financing equipment for Indian construction giants including TISCO, JP Industries and the Jindal group.
he rapid growth and consistent success of Srei in the infrastructure finance domain also attracted top obal players and equipment manufacturers such as Atlas Copco, a reputable Swedish multi-national company.
SREI
Hotel Oberoi Grand, Sunil Kanoria in a eeting with executives of Atlas Copco...
We've been following Srei's achievements and we notice you've been on the honours list for two years in a row.
Thank you. We are really pleased to be associated with Atlas Copco.

In 2003, Srei had been honoured with the Wills Herman Global Award for Spirituality at the Workplace, but the new year brought new challenges.
Of late, many of our competitors have made their way into the space of equipment leasing. As a result, we are losing key customers and prospective clients. The 30% market share that we had painstakingly achieved is under threat.
September 2004... In the Srei boardroom, Hemant is in a meeting with Mr Salil Gupta...

Hemant, competition will always exist; we just need to think out of the box.
True... I was discussing the same with the team the other day. Mr K.K. Mohanty has done some groundwork. We will build on it.

At the next board meeting, Hemant and Sunil chalked out a plan with the support of the team.
The key strategy is to come up with a one-of-a-kind solution. I propose a unique auction event.
You mean an auction for the sale of equipment? What do you have in mind?

The event, inaugurated by Hemant in Kolkata, was a big success.

At the start of the new millennium, the Kanorias had begun the process of realizing their cherished dream of giving back to society through the Srei Foundation.
I was talking to Father the other day. We should create a trust which will be part of our *CSR arm.
*Corporate Social Responsibility
The brothers discussed it with their father, who took the vital step of launching the Srei Foundation.
Apart from that, we can drive health and environmental initiatives that we have been thinking about.
Our primary focus will be empowerment of underprivileged women and children through education and vocational training.
SREI
FOUNDATION
In 2001, the Srei Foundation was established as a recognized philanthropic institution under the chairmanship of Hari Prasad Kanoria, much before the government introduced it as a statute.

In 2005, Hemant and company secretary Sandeep Lakhotia were in London to celebrate another Srei landmark. The company had become one of the first Indian Non-Banking Financial Institutes (NBFIs) to issue a Global Depository Receipt (GDR) and be listed on the London Stock Exchange (LSE).
It is way colder than we thought it would be in London at this time of the year.
Actually, things are specially bad this year.
In London, Hemant and Sandeep were joined by Hemant's younger brother Dr Sanjeev Kanoria.
Being one of the first NBFIs to issue a GDR and being listed on the LSE is an achievement I have long dreamt of.
The Kanoria brothers felt nostalgic, as they remembered driving past the LSE years back....
It is really nice that you will be there with us for the GDR event, Sanjeev.
Wouldn't have missed it for the world!

The Kanoria brothers geared up for the big day...

...spending time planning the GDR issue and press statements.

At the Srei office, D.K. Vyas was talking to a colleague...
Our success at EXCON in Bangalore has created quite a buzz across the country.
Indeed. I was confident we would do well. From what I hear, we registered a record number of transactions. I will get a detailed report tomorrow.

Back in London...
On behalf of the LSE, I extend a warm welcome to you. I called to give you a quick update on the itinerary for the GDR event.

Could you please email me the list of investors and attendees for the press meet?

We want to make the most of this opportunity and promote ourselves globally.
That's great! You can state this at the pre-event press meet.
Sure, we'll address the press. However, we plan to further promote our portfolio to prospective investors.
Well, there are the regular rounds of press releases and media coverage where you can reach out to national and international groups. Do you have a specific target audience? We have a list of global organizations we could help you get in touch with.
Actually, reaching out to the general masses would be a great idea to start with as they are really inclined to invest these days.

Sounds like a plan, gentlemen! I congratulate you in advance and will be glad to assist in any manner possible.

On 21 April 2005, Srei announced its GDR issue amidst applause and celebrations. It was a grand evening. News of Srei's listing on the LSE spread across global media.
Congratulations! I wish you all the best.

Srei Infrastructure Finance Limited
On its Stock Market listing
21 April 2005
LSE then presented Hemant the certificate, marking yet another momentous achievment in the history of Srei.

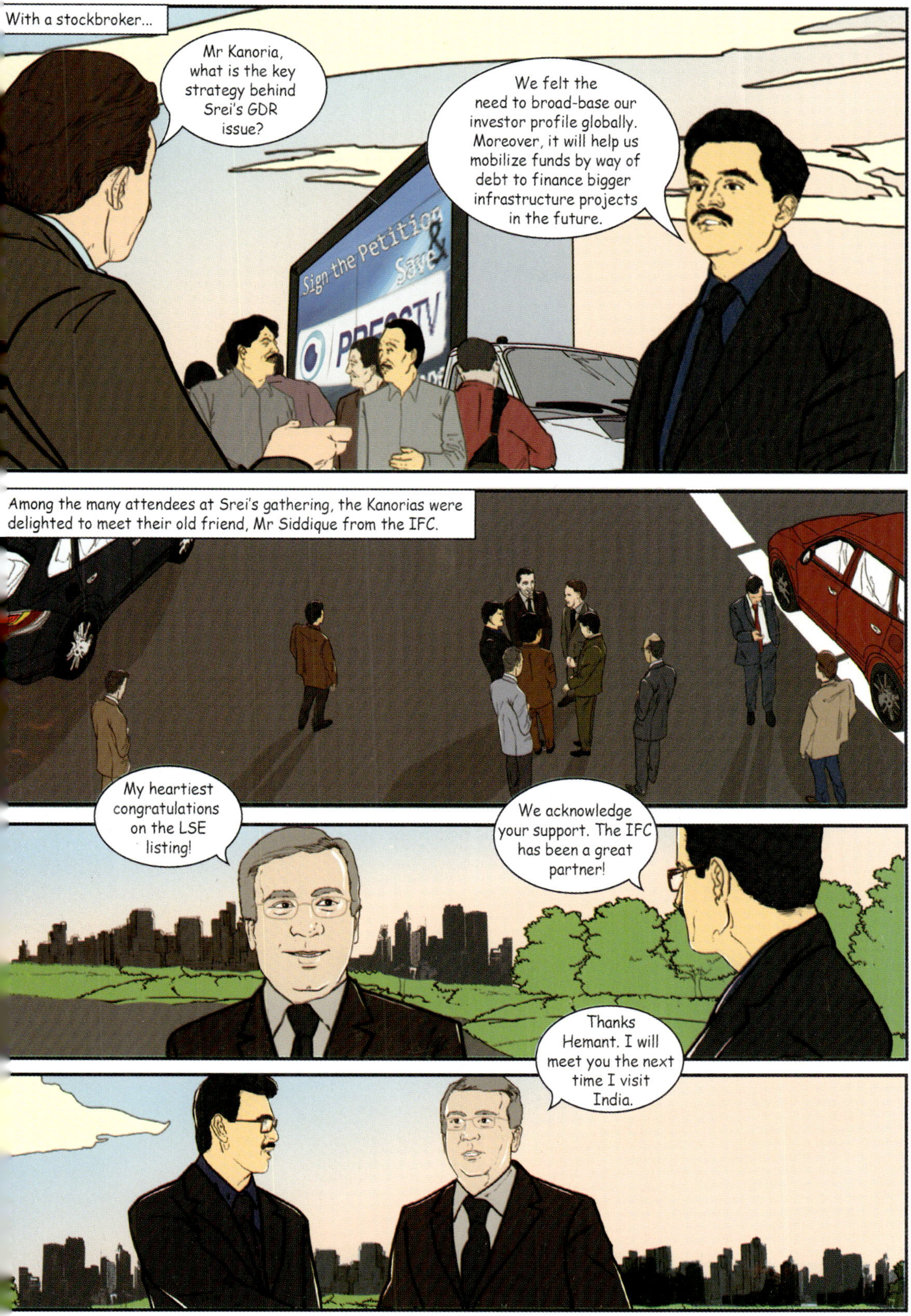

Among the many attendees at Srei's gathering, the Kanorias were delighted to meet their old friend, Mr Siddique from the IFC.

My heartiest congratulations on the LSE listing!

We acknowledge your support. The IFC has been a great partner!

Thanks Hemant. I will meet you the next time I visit India.

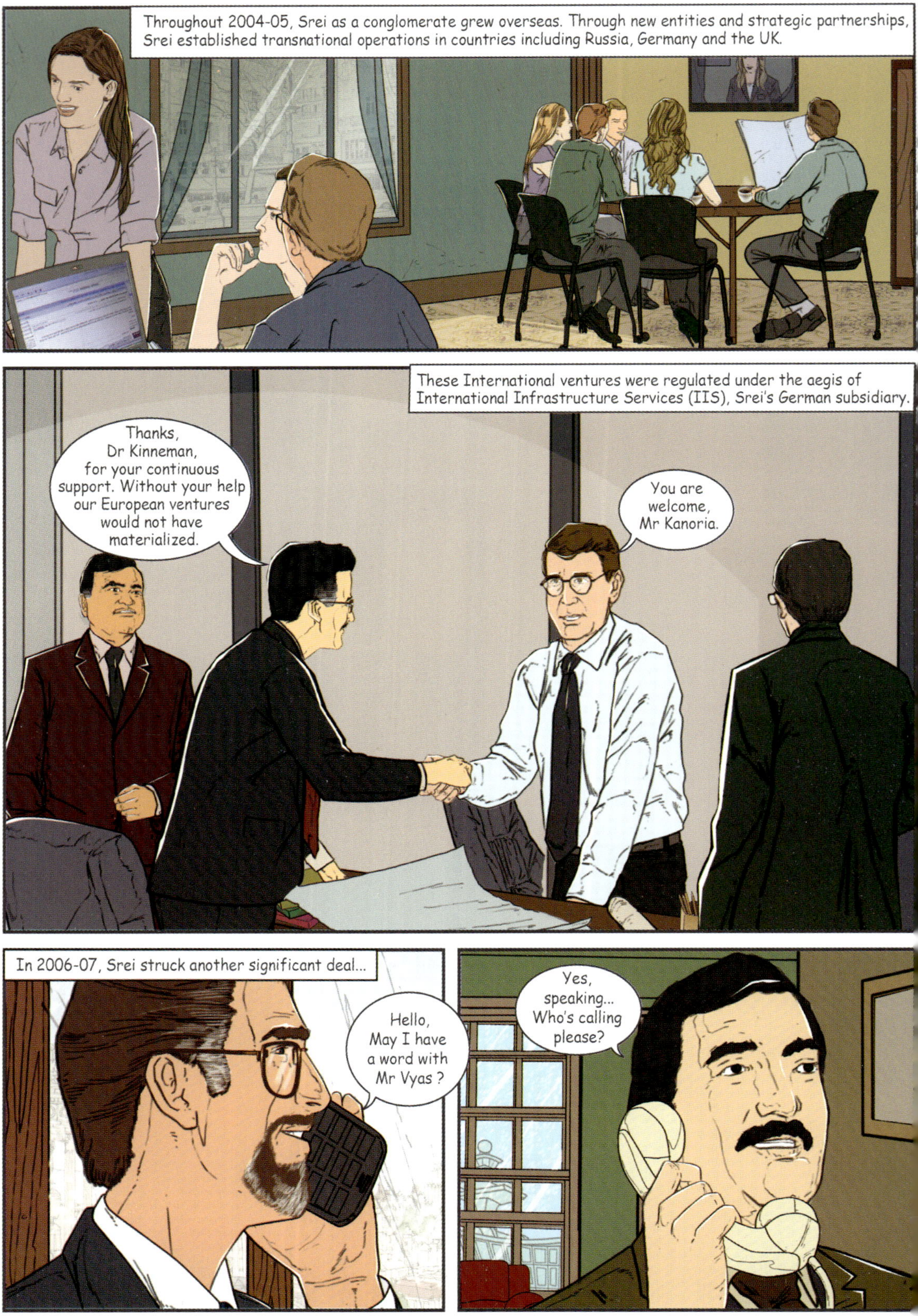

These International ventures were regulated under the aegis of International Infrastructure Services (IIS), Srei's German subsidiary.

Thanks, Dr Kinneman, for your continuous support. Without your help our European ventures would not have materialized.

You are welcome, Mr Kanoria.

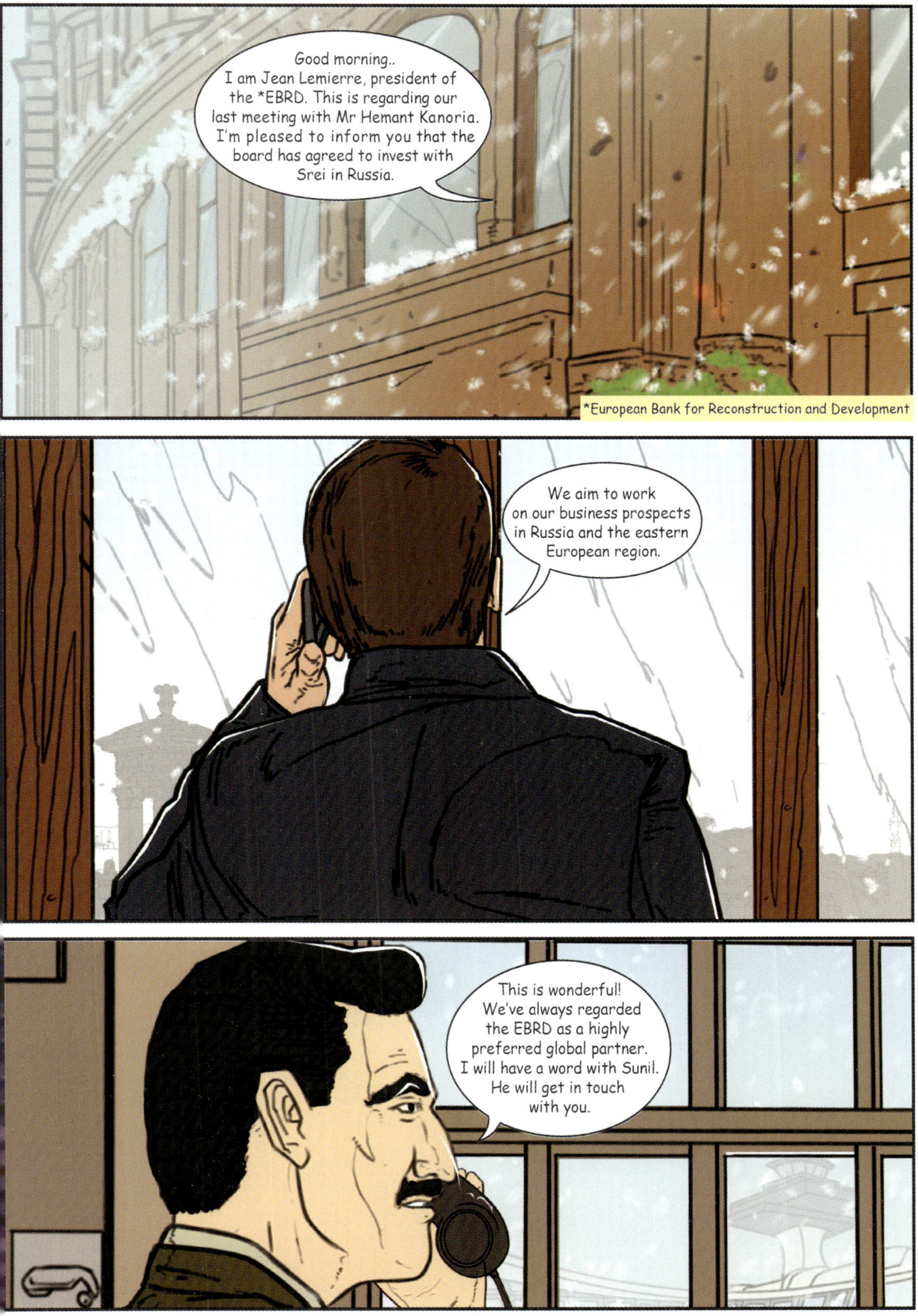

Good morning..
I am Jean Lemierre, president of the *EBRD. This is regarding our last meeting with Mr Hemant Kanoria. I'm pleased to inform you that the board has agreed to invest with Srei in Russia.

*European Bank for Reconstruction and Development

We aim to work on our business prospects in Russia and the eastern European region.

In 2006, Srei entered into partnerships with the EBRD, DEG and the FMO to boost its business prospects.
Congratulations on the launch of Zao Srei Leasing in the Russian market.
Indeed, through Zao Srei, we'll both grow as organizations and provide services in the Russian equipment-financing market, as well as further afield in eastern Europe.
There is a strong buzz about Srei and its accolades globally. What's your key to success in such a short time frame?
Well, we believe in innovation and understanding the dynamics of the market. Our stakeholders are our primary asset and, more importantly, we feel happy about the work we do. The rest follows...

Vithin a short span of time, 'Zao Srei' became a leader in the Russian equipment-financing sector.

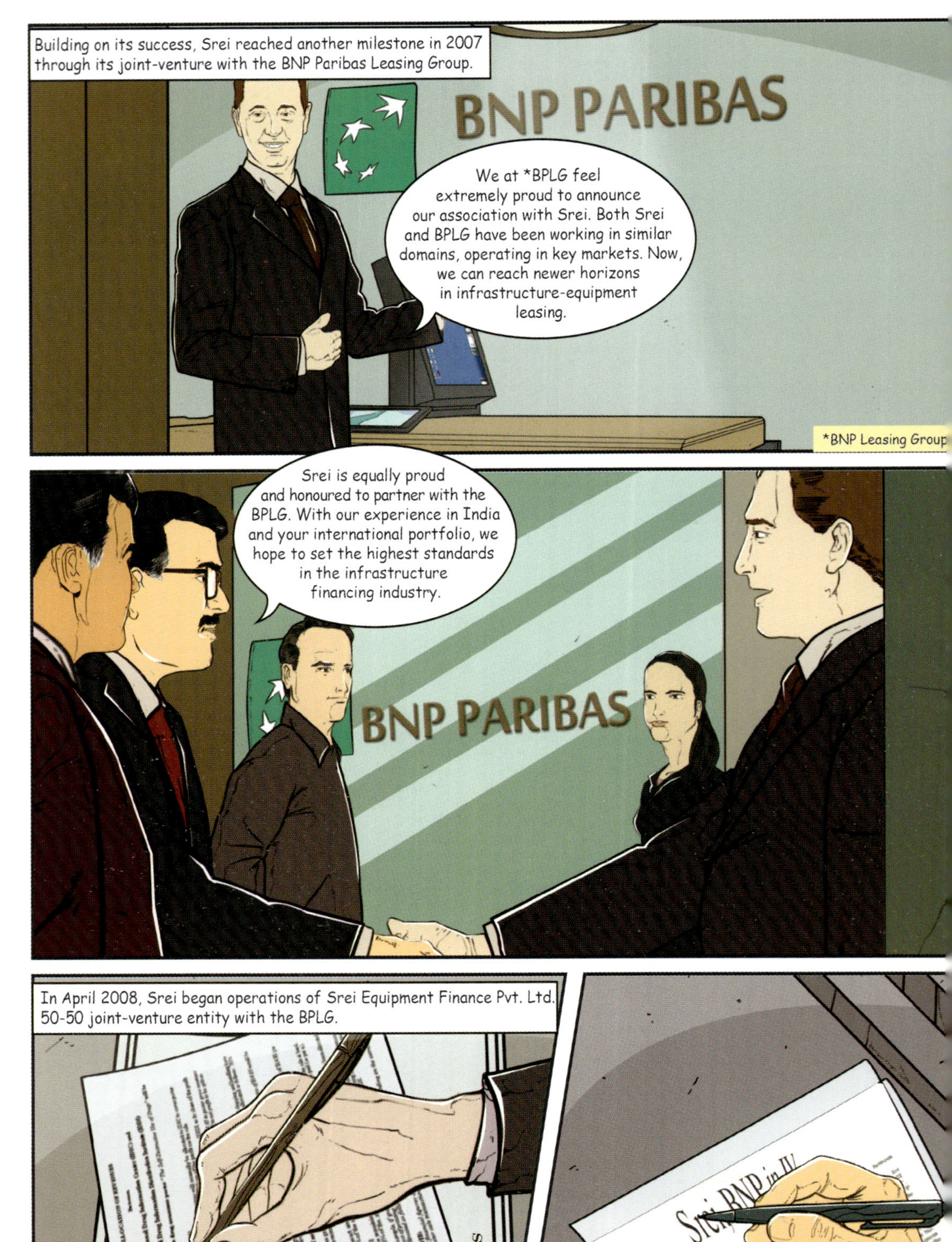
Building on its success, Srei reached another milestone in 2007 through its joint-venture with the BNP Paribas Leasing Group.
BNP PARIBAS
We at *BPLG feel extremely proud to announce our association with Srei. Both Srei and BPLG have been working in similar domains, operating in key markets. Now, we can reach newer horizons in infrastructure-equipment leasing.
*BNP Leasing Group
Srei is equally proud and honoured to partner with the BPLG. With our experience in India and your international portfolio, we hope to set the highest standards in the infrastructure financing industry.
BNP PARIBAS
In April 2008, Srei began operations of Srei Equipment Finance Pvt. Ltd. 50-50 joint-venture entity with the BPLG.
BNP PARIBAS
SREI

The joint-venture added to the capital base of Srei, substantially, and also earned benefits like robust risk management
ractices, access to international customers, clients and manufacturers, and improved access to global vendors.

Srei and the BPLG quickly went on to partner with the biggest equipment manufacturers
and technology players in the world, with D.K. Vyas at the helm of affairs.
SREI

n early 2008, the Kanorias bought the telecom tower arm of Spice Telecom
hrough their telecom arm, Quippo Telecom International Limited (QTIL).
During a visit to their Punjab power facility, Sunil was greeted by B.K. Modi, chairman of Spice Telecom.
Sunil, each of these telecom towers amount to Rs 70 lakh. I'm sure QTIL will help fulfil our dream of connecting rural and urban India with a simple phone call.
WB-3443

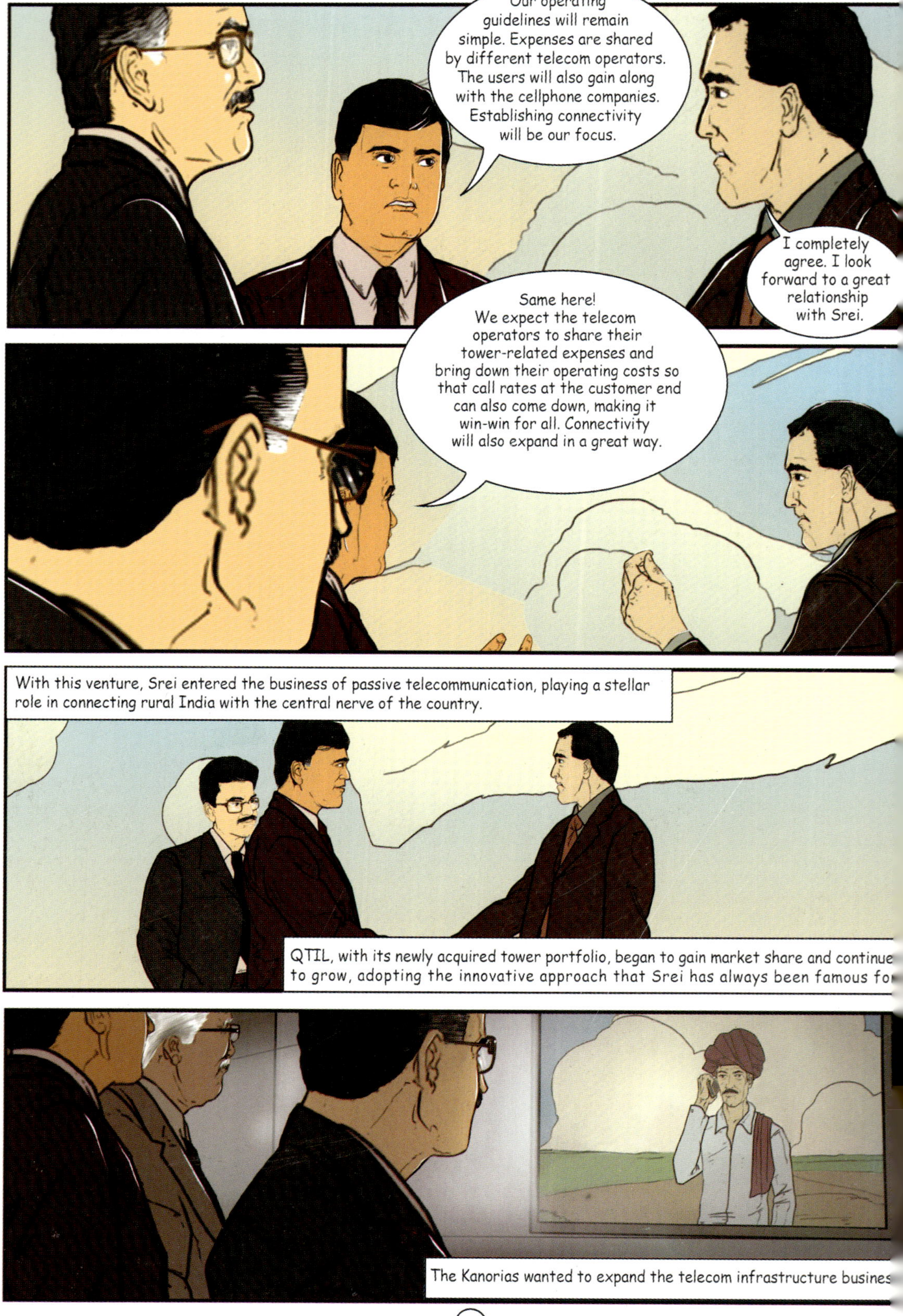

Our operating guidelines will remain simple. Expenses are shared by different telecom operators. The users will also gain along with the cellphone companies. Establishing connectivity will be our focus.

I completely agree. I look forward to a great relationship with Srei.

Same here! We expect the telecom operators to share their tower-related expenses and bring down their operating costs so that call rates at the customer end can also come down, making it win-win for all. Connectivity will also expand in a great way.

With this venture, Srei entered the business of passive telecommunication, playing a stellar role in connecting rural India with the central nerve of the country.

QTIL, with its newly acquired tower portfolio, began to gain market share and continue to grow, adopting the innovative approach that Srei has always been famous fo

A few months later, Sunil received a call from Arun Kapur at his office. As he spoke, Sunil's excitement was subtle, but evident.
Tata Teleservices... Hmm...Thanks Arun. Let me discuss this with Hemant. Keep me updated.
Later...
Arun just called... The Tatas want to demerge their telecom tower business and divest 49% of their stake.
So we'll be bidding against the big boys in telecom... Do you think we can get this?
As they headed out for a meeting, the discussion continued in the car...
Hemant, our portfolio of 1,000 telecom towers in Punjab and Haryana gives us an edge. Besides, we'll pitch better.

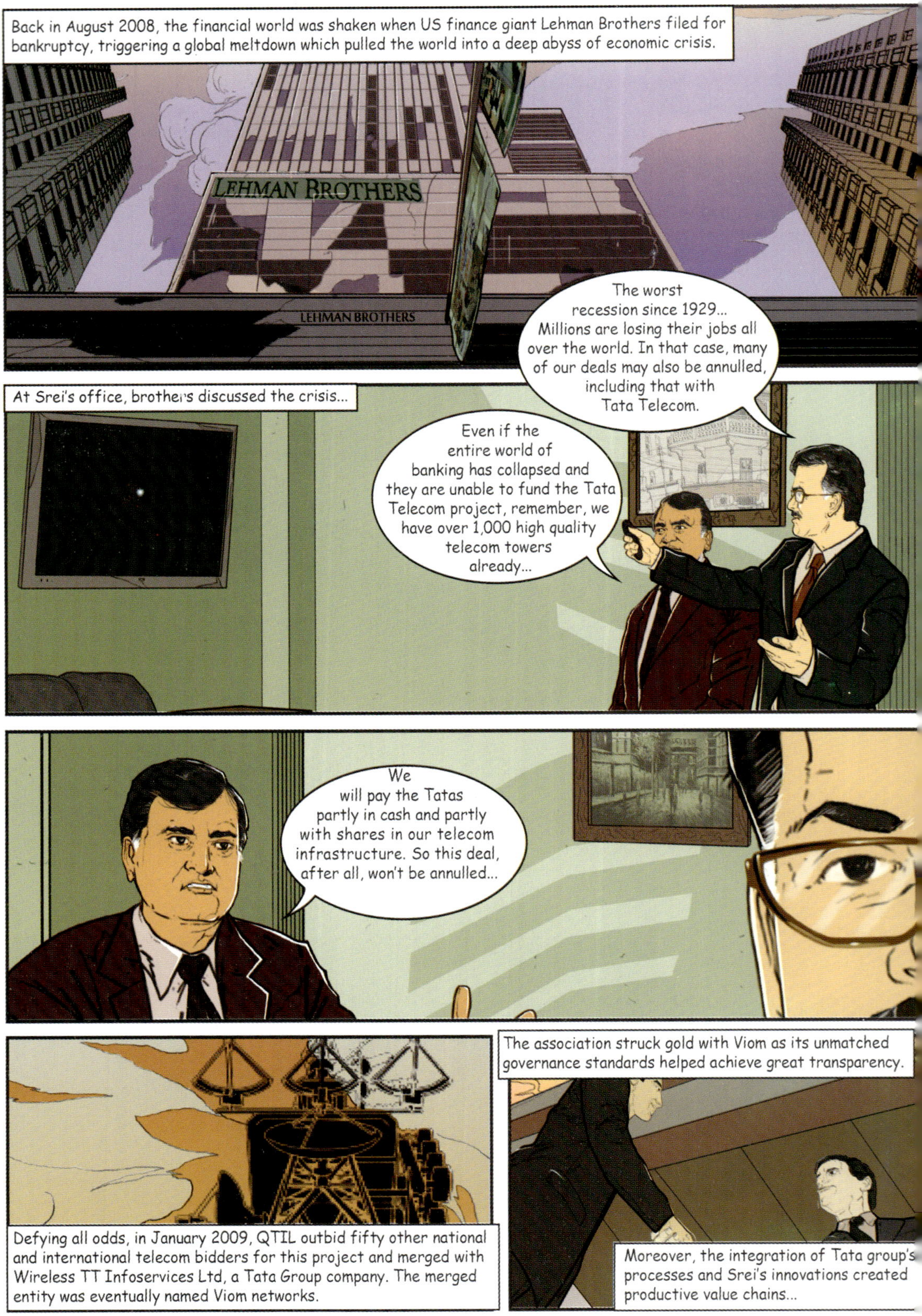

Back in August 2008, the financial world was shaken when US finance giant Lehman Brothers filed for bankruptcy, triggering a global meltdown which pulled the world into a deep abyss of economic crisis.

LEHMAN BROTHERS

LEHMAN BROTHERS

The worst recession since 1929... Millions are losing their jobs all over the world. In that case, many of our deals may also be annulled, including that with Tata Telecom.

At Srei's office, brothers discussed the crisis...

Even if the entire world of banking has collapsed and they are unable to fund the Tata Telecom project, remember, we have over 1,000 high quality telecom towers already...

Defying all odds, in January 2009, QTIL outbid fifty other national and international telecom bidders for this project and merged with Wireless TT Infoservices Ltd, a Tata Group company. The merged entity was eventually named Viom networks.

The association struck gold with Viom as its unmatched governance standards helped achieve great transparency.

As 2010 drew to a close, Srei's rapid growth continued as it invested in DPSC through Indian Power Corporation Limited (IPCL)...

...and subsequently ventured into energy rental...

...and also in gas-based power through Quippo Energy Pvt. Ltd.

Srei amalgamated the IPCL with the DPSC...
A heritage company, the DPSC functioned in power generation, transmission and distribution in the industrial belt of Asansol in West Bengal.

In late 2010, Srei, through its brand Attivo, ventured into the business of developing industrial parks across India.
Simultaneously, Srei ventured into new asset classes, such as wind energy, IT hardware and software, and healthcare equipment.
In 2010-11, Srei was awarded infrastructure finance company status by the RBI.

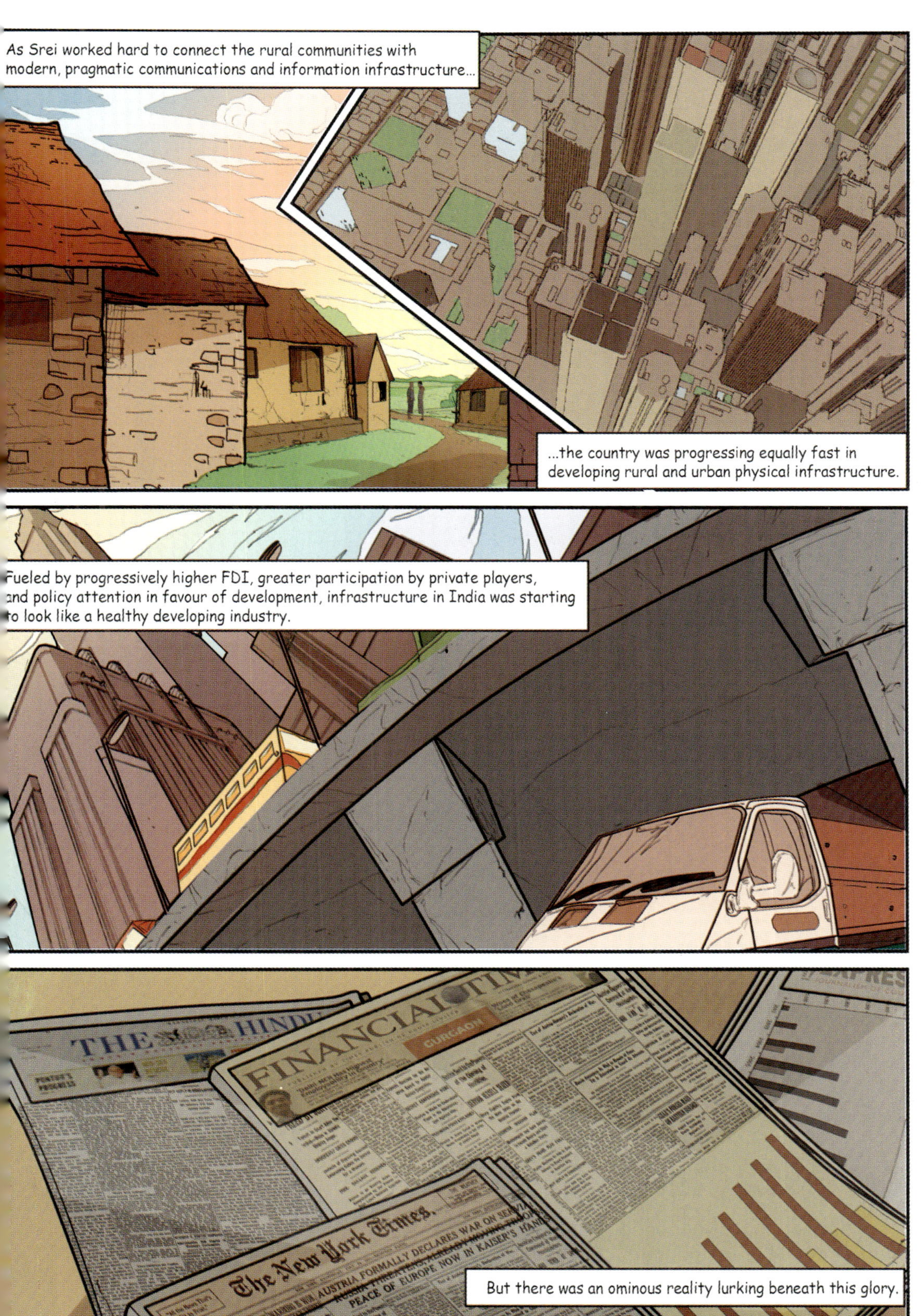
As Srei worked hard to connect the rural communities with modern, pragmatic communications and information infrastructure...
...the country was progressing equally fast in developing rural and urban physical infrastructure.
Fueled by progressively higher FDI, greater participation by private players, and policy attention in favour of development, infrastructure in India was starting to look like a healthy developing industry.
But there was an ominous reality lurking beneath this glory.

By 2012, the government spiralled downwards due to many problems.
The national media buzzed with headlines on multiple controversies and deficits in administrative functions...
The impact on governance affected development, culminating in policy paralysis within the market.
NO VACANCY
As the problems of the government increased, the country spiralled into an economic abyss, characterized by a menacing slowdown in infrastructure and other sectors.

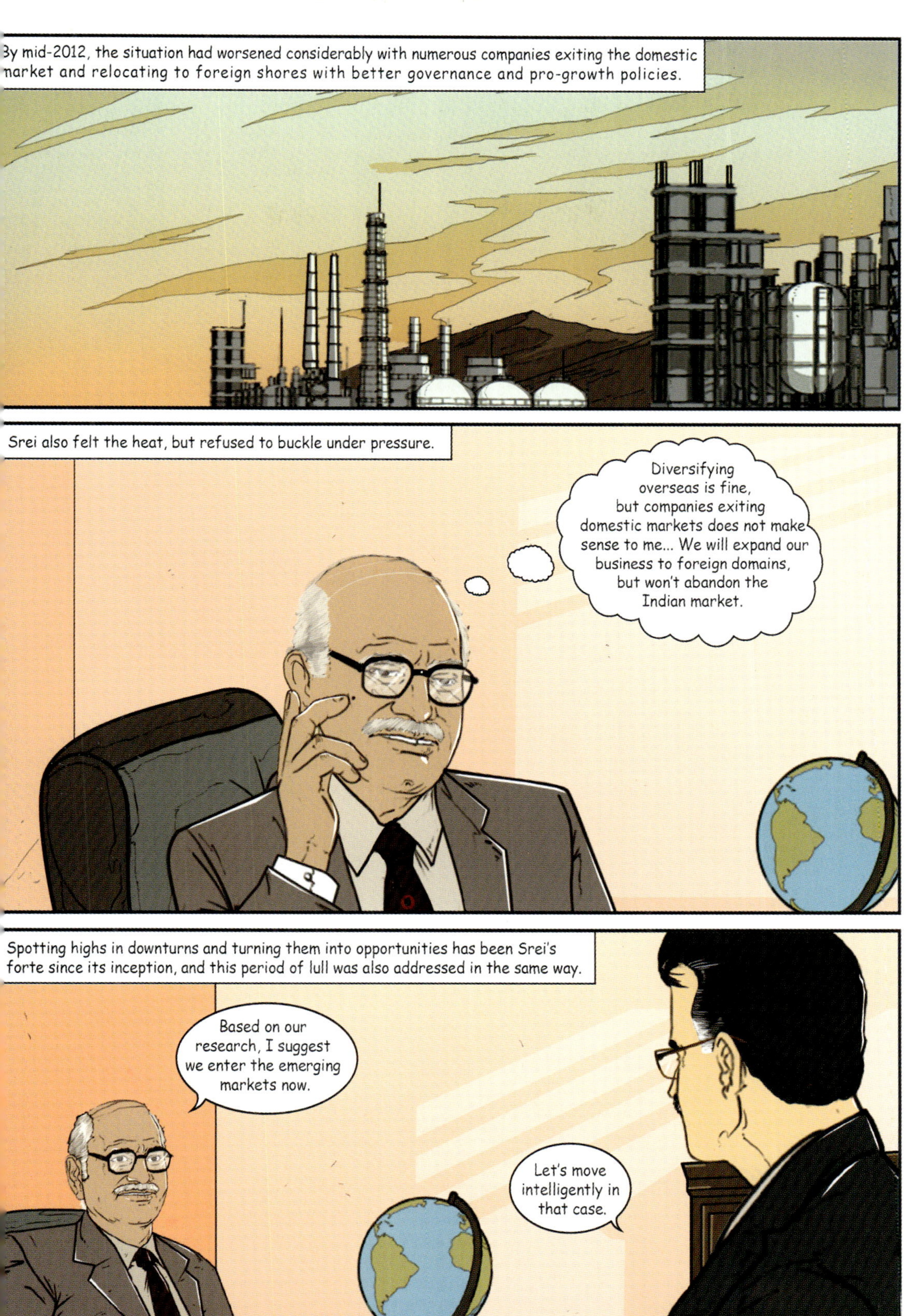
By mid-2012, the situation had worsened considerably with numerous companies exiting the domestic market and relocating to foreign shores with better governance and pro-growth policies.
Srei also felt the heat, but refused to buckle under pressure.
Diversifying overseas is fine, but companies exiting domestic markets does not make sense to me... We will expand our business to foreign domains, but won't abandon the Indian market.
Spotting highs in downturns and turning them into opportunities has been Srei's forte since its inception, and this period of lull was also addressed in the same way.
Based on our research, I suggest we enter the emerging markets now.
Let's move intelligently in that case.

In 2007-08, the government approved the National e-Governance Plan (NeGP), whose ultimate objective is to bring public services closer home to citizens, even in the remotest village.
This new initiative gives us an opportunity to bridge the urban-rural digital divide.
If we can extend Internet-enabled services to the rural hinterlands, we can also encourage village-based entrepreneurs.
Hmm... This facility can be used for e-governance, e-commerc and e-learning...and this, in tur will lead to more jobs.
This liquidity would create more village-based entrepreneurs who can run Internet kiosks.
I see unique scope in the areas of agriculture, education, vocational training, health and hygiene.
As Father says, the most complex of problems have the simplest of solutions, that's Sahaj for us.
SAHAJ
वसुधा केन्द्र
Sahaj e-Village, today, is the largest rural IT infrastructure initiative in India, with 52,442 Common Service Centres catering to roughly 450 million rural Indians in twenty-two states, imparting Business to Business, Business to Consumer, Government to Citizen services and e-learning courses.

The employment portal Chaakri.in, under the Sahaj e-Village initiative, provides sustainable livelihood to under-skilled villagers.
Such programmes have facilitated direct interaction between the employer and employees in a number of states, including Assam, Bihar, Odisha, Tamil Nadu, Uttar Pradesh and West Bengal.
In 2011, Srei Infrastructure Finance launched Swachh Environment Pvt. Ltd. an environmental engineering management initiative focused on integrated waste management, pollution monitoring, water and waste-water treatment, and hazardous and industrial waste collection.
In 2012, Srei entered into a joint-venture with Veolia, a global leader in water infrastructure, through Swachh. Veolia and Swachh were awarded the fifteen-year Nangloi PPP contract, designed to supply clean water to 1 million inhabitants of Nangloi, West Delhi. It is the capital's largest PPP project in the water sector.

In 2014, Srei felt the need to bring its numerous organizations under one umbrella...
Kanoria Foundation
WORK WITH DEVOTION
The Kanoria Foundation is a trust entity dedicated to the development of society with the creation of business enterprises that have long-term and sustainable objectives.

The Kanoria Foundation also brought the bloodline into action as Mukund, Anant and Raghav, the children of Sanjeev, Sunil and Hemant, respectively, prepared to take the legacy forward...
The Kanoria family plays a key role in steering the organization under the Kanoria Foundation.

Dr Sanjeev Kanoria spearheads SUASTH Healthcare, which is responsible for establishing hospitals.

youngest of the four brothers, oversees the Kanoria
hospitality and housing infrastructure projects.
His interest in technology, innovation and design have led him to take on some of the most creative projects for the foundation, including affordable housing, smart cities and sustainable urban development, as well as the more traditional commercial projects.

The Kanoria Foundation aptly mirrors the holistic approach and spiritual ethos which form the backbone of Srei. The wisdom of Hari Prasad Kanoria, the vision of his sons, and the energy of the progeny combine into a force which successfully drives this initiative.

As Srei marched ahead on the social and business fronts, India elected a *BJP-led government in 2014.
LIVE
DTV
BREAKING NEWS
Narendra Modi took oath at the Rashtrapati Bhavan and his promise of 'Better Days' resounded within the economy.
*Bharatiya Janata Party

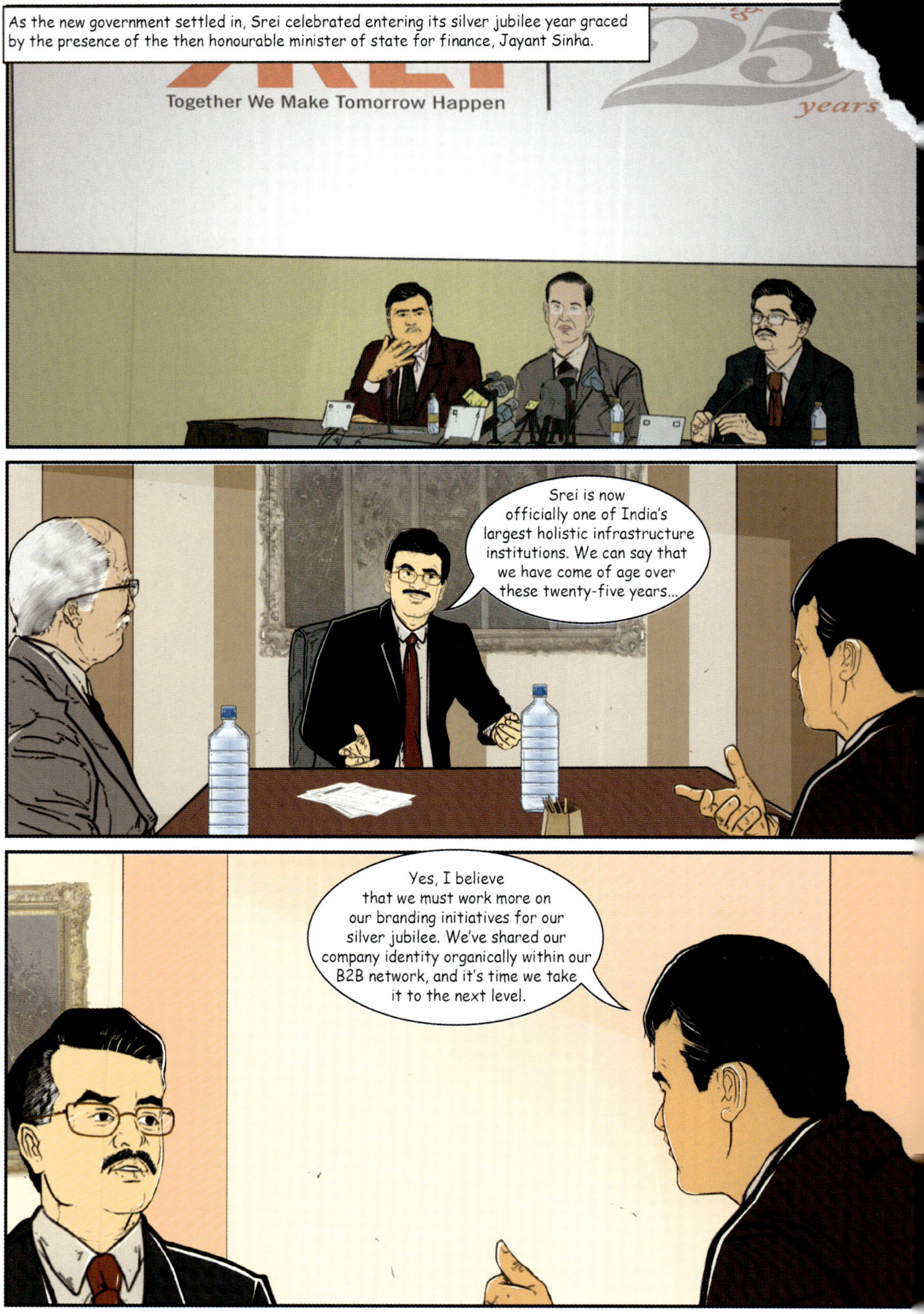

As the new government settled in, Srei celebrated entering its silver jubilee year graced by the presence of the then honourable minister of state for finance, Jayant Sinha.

Together We Make Tomorrow Happen

25 years

Srei is now officially one of India's largest holistic infrastructure institutions. We can say that we have come of age over these twenty-five years...

Right, we must focus on communicating our brand identity. Srei has a global presence with multiple service areas, which directly or indirectly touch lives on a daily basis.

Later that day, Mukund, Anant and Raghav, the next generation of the Kanoria family also shared their inputs...
We want to express a thought regarding our branding.
The company is looking at its twenty-fifth year now, so why don't we reflect it by reinventing our tagline?
Yes... This is a way to express to our partners, clients, customers and stakeholders that we will keep moving ahead together.
Something more inclusive like 'Together we make tomorrow happen'?
Great! 'Together we make tomorrow happen' sounds perfect.

As Srei completes twenty-five years, it covers an illustrious journey characterized by towering highs and challenging lows...

The Kanorias are far from complacent and their zeal to take on new chal
converting every hurdle into a new opportunity keeps growing stronger e

Riding high on the recent wave of change, their congruity with the new government's plans of inclusive growth and improved standards of living, the Kanorias are determined to elevate Indian infrastructure...

...and live up to the name of Srei, meaning 'shrestha' or 'the best'.

ei foundation has expanded its social
tivities in the last sixteen years...
The 'World Confluence of Humanity, Power & Spirituality' is a unique annual event conceptualised to strengthen the spiritual fabric of the society and create awareness about the power of the human soul, which is spearheaded by H.P. Kanoria and Champa Devi.
he Srei India Scholarship Fund of $ 50,000 in collaboration with Boston University finances talented students from across the world.
Institute for Inspiration and Self-Development (IISD) runs various professional, management, entrepreneurship and competitive programmes to promote higher education. It also offers financial support to students, who require it. Madhulika Kanoria, vice chairman of IISD, has been instrumental in introducing PGDM courses with affiliation to the All India Management Association (AIMA).
Sangita Kanoria looks after the healthcare activities of the foundation.
Education and skill development for underprivileged slum children through Suryodaya Schools, jointly managed by the Suryodaya Trust and the Srei Foundation, under chief patron Sunita Kanoria.
Acid Survivors Foundation of India (AFSI) provides country-wide support to victims of acid attacks, largely women, and generates awareness about violence against women, under the stewardship of Divita Kanoria, who also manages the Vedic Collection, a range of organic wellness products.
Adoption of fifteen 'one-teacher schools' in Gaya district of Bihar to provide informal education among tribal communities.
Manisha Lohia is the founder and managing editor of Ispark—a children's educational magazine.
he Srei Foundation has undertaken various nitiatives to clean the environment, rimarily waterbodies.
Shruti Kanoria is the vice chairman of Business Economics, a renowned holistic magazine run by the Kanoria Foundation.
Project Akshar is an initiative to maximize the use of waste paper.
Viom Networks has undertaken plantation drives in various parts of the country.

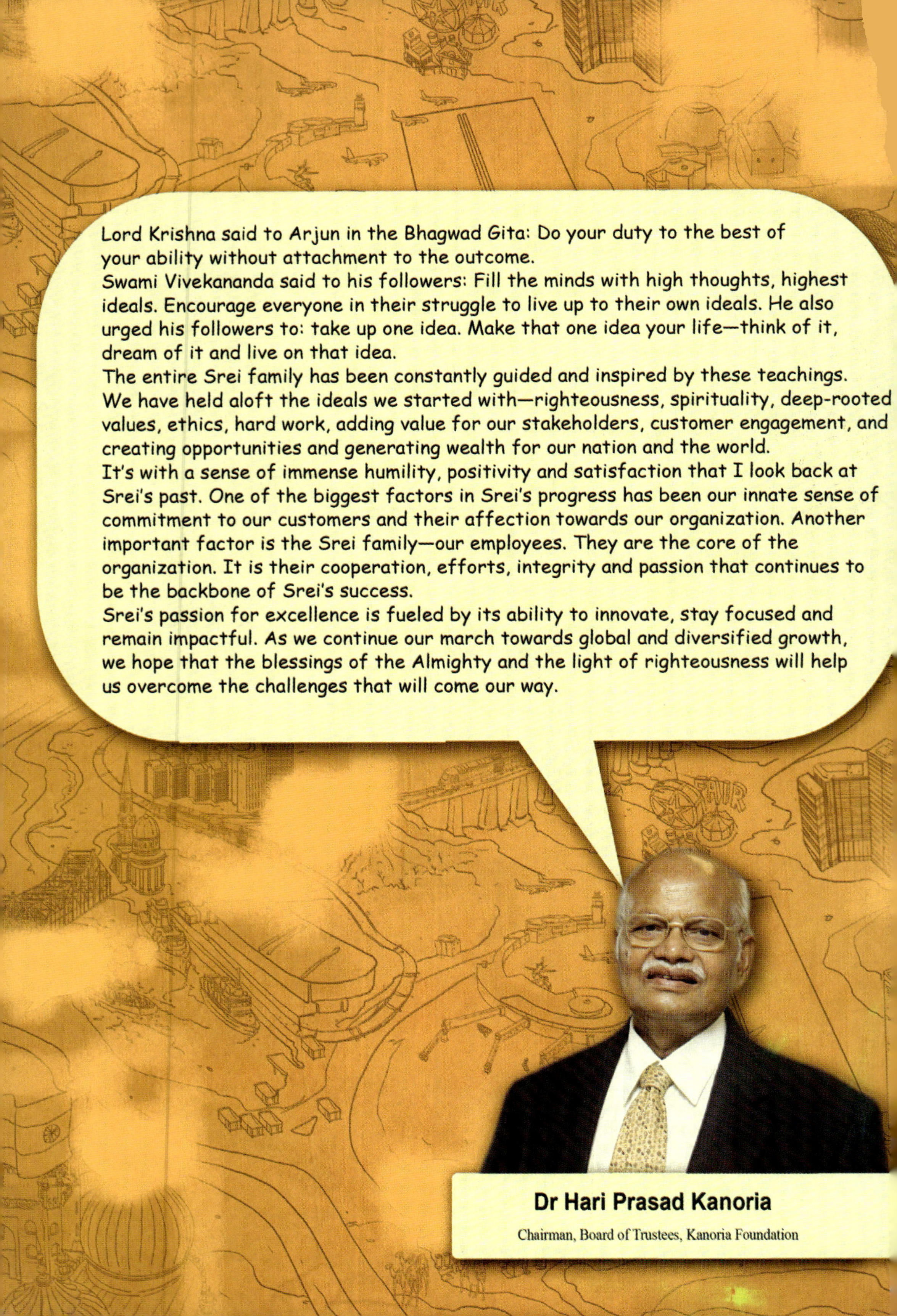
Lord Krishna said to Arjun in the Bhagwad Gita: Do your duty to the best of your ability without attachment to the outcome.
Swami Vivekananda said to his followers: Fill the minds with high thoughts, highest ideals. Encourage everyone in their struggle to live up to their own ideals. He also urged his followers to: take up one idea. Make that one idea your life—think of it, dream of it and live on that idea.
The entire Srei family has been constantly guided and inspired by these teachings. We have held aloft the ideals we started with—righteousness, spirituality, deep-rooted values, ethics, hard work, adding value for our stakeholders, customer engagement, and creating opportunities and generating wealth for our nation and the world.
It's with a sense of immense humility, positivity and satisfaction that I look back at Srei's past. One of the biggest factors in Srei's progress has been our innate sense of commitment to our customers and their affection towards our organization. Another important factor is the Srei family—our employees. They are the core of the organization. It is their cooperation, efforts, integrity and passion that continues to be the backbone of Srei's success.
Srei's passion for excellence is fueled by its ability to innovate, stay focused and remain impactful. As we continue our march towards global and diversified growth, we hope that the blessings of the Almighty and the light of righteousness will help us overcome the challenges that will come our way.
Dr Hari Prasad Kanoria
Chairman, Board of Trustees, Kanoria Foundation

In the last quarter of a century, India has created a pioneering model to develop infrastructure through the length and breadth of our country. While the government has been making investments and building world-class infrastructure, it has been able to attract private sector companies and investments to structure innovative PPPs in infrastructure—from roads to airport, power, ports, industrial parks, water and so on.

Srei has been a child of this dream, commencing our journey in the infrastructure sector about twenty-six years back, we have grown our businesses hand in hand with the government's dream of making India one of the strongest nations in the world. Both, the country and Srei, have had their set of successes and failures. We have learnt a lot, achieved many a laurel and we are on our journey to fulfil more dreams in the years to come. As they say 'the sky is the limit' and in this sector, it is truly so.

HEMANT KANORIA
Chairman & Managing Director

We started out in 1989 with a dream to see India at the best of its infrastructure, and it is only now that I realize how far we have come in these twenty-six years. Srei is one of the few private infrastructure players to have worked closely alongside the government through its infrastructure journey, making India one of the leaders in sectors such as aviation, ports, roads, telecom and power, among others.

This book aims to capture the various stages of infrastructure growth post-independence, and how we as an organization played a small, yet significant role through this transformation. It tells the story of the ups and downs, and captures the details of our hardships and laurels. We hope this book serves as an inspiration for all young enthusiastic entrepreneurs, who, like us, have a dream and are looking for a way to fulfil it.

We hope our story inspires you to take your ideas to greater heights and more importantly helps you create your own story.

SUNIL KANORIA
Vice Chairman

I extend my good wishes to the Srei family for having completed twenty-five years of operations and emerging as one of the leaders in the industry. India's infrastructure journey over the past few decades has gone through a series of ups and downs. But it has maintained its quest to make India a global economic superpower, starting from the opening up of the economy to facing external challenges head-on. Innovation and the ability to take risk are key to long-term sustainability. It is important to remember that while it may be relatively easy to maintain these values during good times, the true test of a company comes only when it is faced with tough challenges. Having faced and overcome some difficult hurdles, Srei has emerged stronger than ever. It gives me great pleasure to recommend this book as an example of what a group of individuals can achieve through determination and hard work.
JAYANT SINHA
Hon'ble Minister of State
for Civil Aviation